Sufferings of Union Soldiers in Southern Prisons

TRANSCRIPT OF THE ANDERSONVILLE TRIAL

Samuel J. M. Andrews

A SECTION FROM THE EAST SIDE OF THE PRISON SHOWING THE DEAD LINE

WITH
NEW INTRODUCTION AND INDEX
BY
Helen Cox Tregillis

HERITAGE BOOKS
2011

HERITAGE BOOKS

AN IMPRINT OF HERITAGE BOOKS, INC.

Books, CDs, and more—Worldwide

For our listing of thousands of titles see our website
at
www.HeritageBooks.com

A Facsimile Reprint
Published 2011 by
HERITAGE BOOKS, INC.
Publishing Division
100 Railroad Ave. #104
Westminster, Maryland 21157

— Publisher's Notice —
In reprints such as this, it is often not possible to remove blemishes from
the original. We feel the contents of this book warrant its reissue despite
these blemishes and hope you will agree and read it with pleasure.

International Standard Book Numbers
Paperbound: 978-0-7884-0573-0
Clothbound: 978-0-7884-8607-4

CONTENTS

INTRODUCTION

by Helen Cox Tregillis

After discovering this booklet at a small local library, I immediately wondered who this Samuel J. M. Andrews was and why he had this particular work published. I soon learned. He lived that nightmare and was a witness during the trial of Henry Wirz for the horrors committed at Andersonville.

Samuel John Mills Andrews was born 22 March, 1836, in Clayton, Adams County, Illinois, the son of Amos Andrews and Roxy Cordelia Taylor. On 25 May, 1861, he enlisted in Company E of the 17th Illinois Regiment, being a resident of Galesbury, Illinois, at that time.

Andrews was mustered in at Peoria, Illinois, and left camp on the 17th of June for Alton, Illinois, until the regiment was completely ready. Late in July, he proceeded from Alton to St. Charles, Missouri, for one day before he went to Warrenton, Missouri, where he remained in camp for two weeks.

He and his regiment were involved in various engagements in which many men were wounded and killed. During the two-day battle toward Corinth, his regiment lost some 130 killed and wounded. After the evacuation of Corinth, he marched to Purdy, Bethel and Jackson, Tennessee, and remained there until July 17 when the regiment was ordered to Bolivar, Mississippi, for assignment as provost guard. In November, 1862, he and his regiment proceeded to other locations.

On January 16, 1863, he, with the others, went to Vicksburg, Mississippi, which became the headquarters of the 17th army corps until the term of service expired on 24

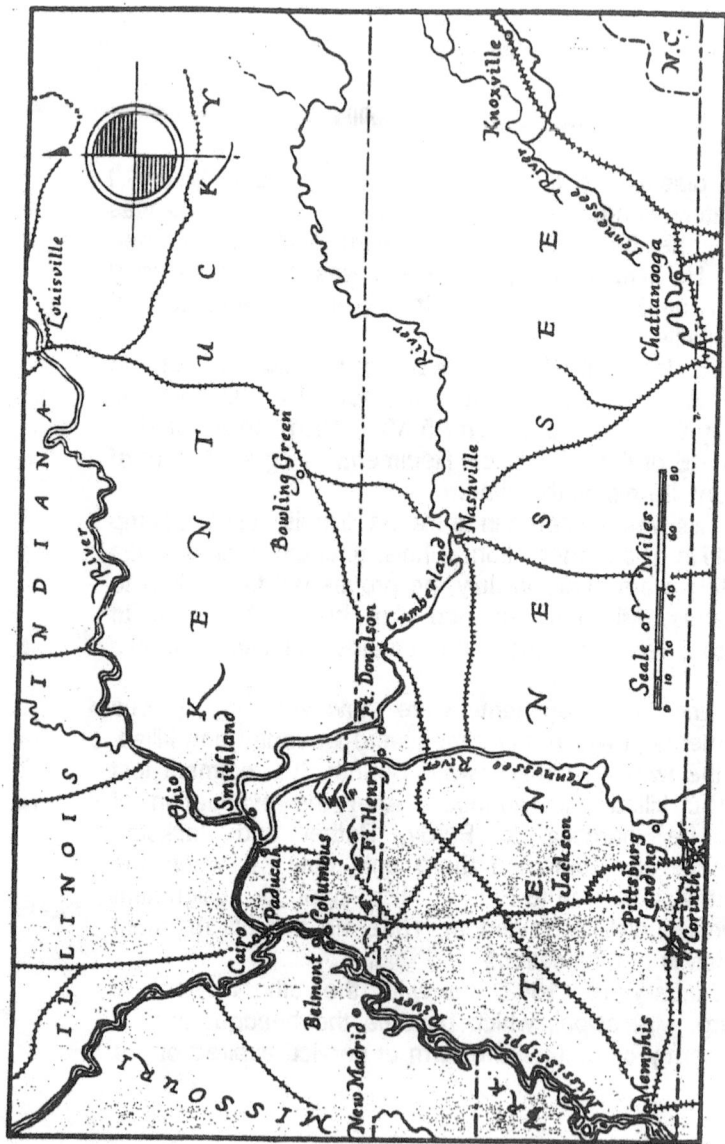

A star marks the site of Corinth where Andrews and the 17th Illinois fought in 1861 before moving on to Tennessee.

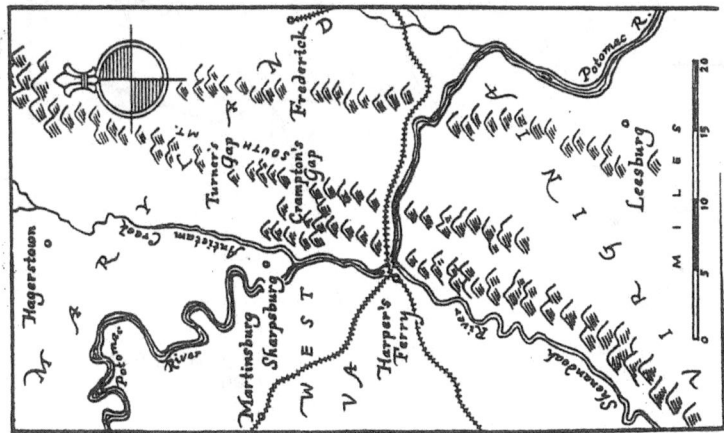

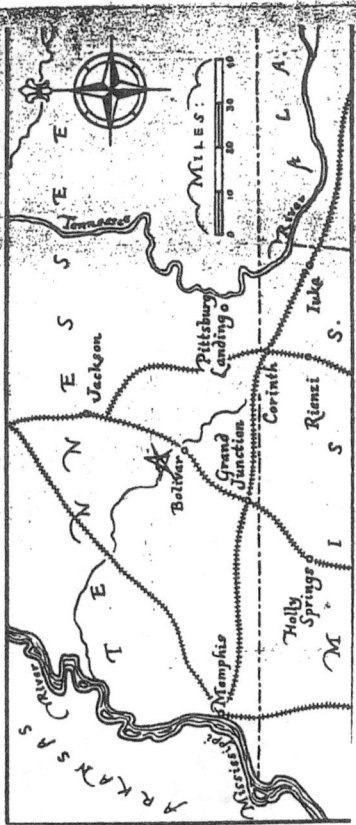

Andrews and the 17th Illinois regiment moved on to Bolivar, Tennessee after their initial action at Corinth near the Tennessee–Mississippi border.

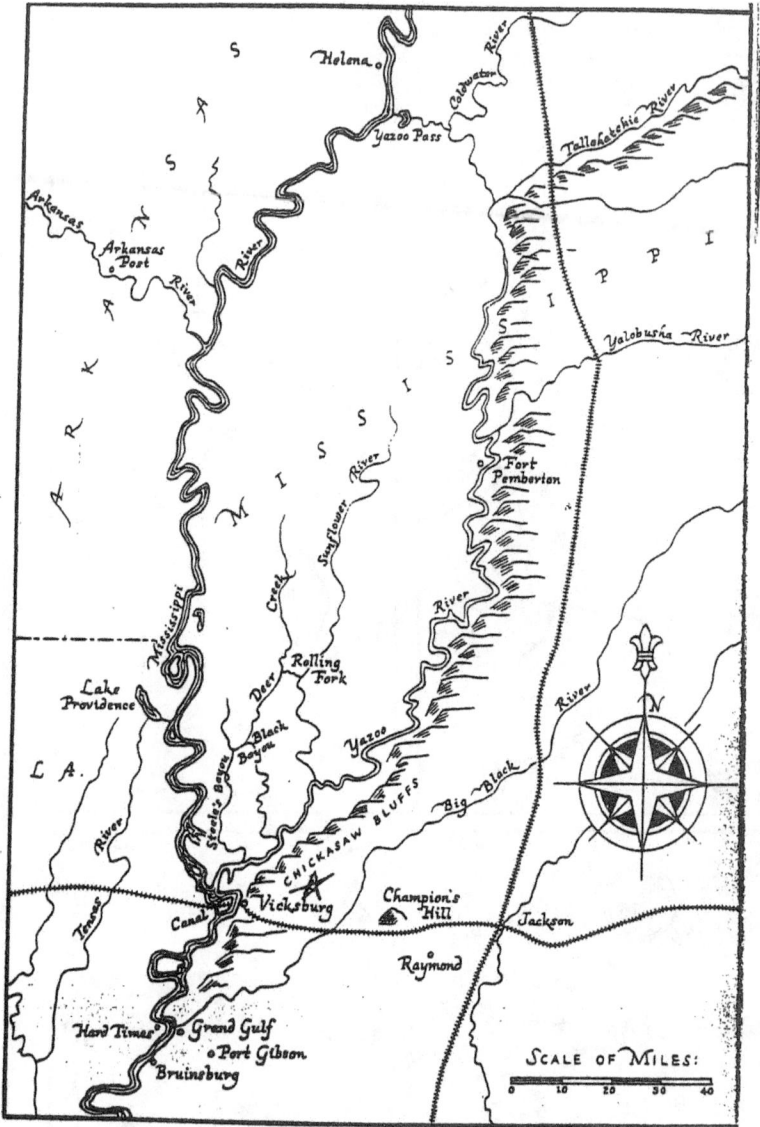

Vicksburg, Mississippi became the headquarters of the 17th army corps in 1863 where many Union movements were made into enemy territory.

May, 1864. Andrews and others made incursions into the enemy's country as far west as Monroe, Louisiana. In March, 1864, the 17th Illinois was consolidated with the 8th Illinois so that the unit was strengthened at Vicksburg. It may be probable that on one of the movements that began on July 1, 1864, under the command of General Elias S. Dennis to Jackson, Mississippi, that Andrews was captured. When the men returned to Vicksburg, it was reported that 3 men were killed, 21 wounded, and two were missing. Andrews may have been one of those missing.

Andrews spent nearly a year in the southern Confederate prisons, one of them being Andersonville or Camp Sumter. The prison had been hastily built in February, 1864, when overcrowding threatened the safety at Richmond. Originally designed to hold 10,000 inmates, the prison was a log stockade of 16 and 1/2 acres (later enlarged to 26 acres) with a stream of water running through it.

Rations were the same as those of the Confederate soldiers in the field: cornmeal, beans and rarely meat. Within the first month of captivity, the prisoners' bodies would begin to deteriorate. Their gums would soften, teeth fall out and dysentery would set in.

The large number of inmates did not aid sanitary conditions in the stockade. Latrines were placed on slopes everywhere, and the excreta was allowed to run down into the only water supply of the stockade.

Medical treatment was almost nonexistent as southern doctors were unwilling to enter the stockade to treat the prisoners. The scurvy, diarrhea, dysentery and gangrene prevailed by mid-year, 1864. All the doctors could do was complain.

Only enlisted men were confined at Andersonville, and in the summer of 1864, the number totaled 32,899. Number of those who died is unknown but there are some 12,912 graves in the cemetery.

Andrews mentioned the execution of six men that took place in July, 1864. Factions developed within the ranks of the inmates into two sides: N'Yaarkers or Raiders vs. the Regulators. The Raiders would pressure any new prisoners to give up food and whatever else they possessed. The

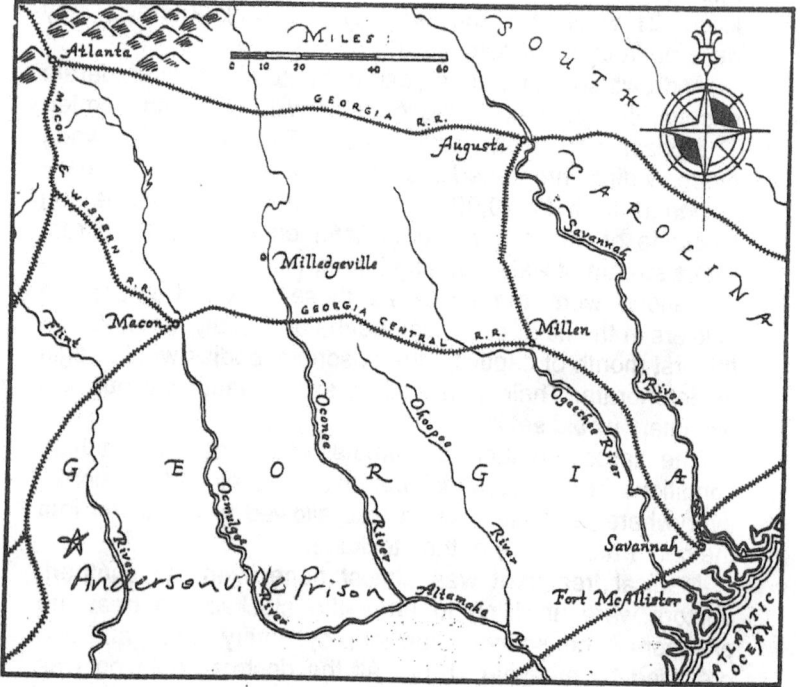

Andersonville Prison or Camp Sumpter became the rallying cause for reprisal after the end of the war. Henry Wirz' death was the only one resulting from trial for war crimes.

Regulators organized, specifically under the guise of some prisoners from Illinois who led the squelching of the N'Yaarkers. Wirz sanctioned the trial among the prisoners, and as a consequence, six of the N'Yaarkers were hanged and buried in a separate plot from the rest.

In September, 1864, when General Sherman approached the area of Andersonville, the well prisoners were sent to Charleston. By then the Confederate officials had already begun an inquiry into the conditions at Andersonville under the command of Captain Henry Wirz.

Captain Henry Wirz, a native-born Swiss, had practiced medicine in Louisiana and was a clerk in the Libby prison early in the war. He was wounded at Seven Pines, and after recovery, he was promoted to captain. At General John Henry Winder's instigation, Jefferson Davis sent Wirz to Europe as a Confederate agent and dispatch bearer. When Wirz returned to the United States, he was appointed commandant of the Andersonville prison which was created in January, 1864.

General John Henry Winder was in charge of all Confederate prisons east of the Mississippi. He died of fatigue and strain in February, 1865. As a consequence, he escaped the death penalty which was dispensed on Henry Wirz in November, 1865. Public sentiment resulted in a "witch hunt" to find those responsible for the conditions at Andersonville. The military trial took place in Washington, D.C., where many individuals testified against Captain Henry Wirz, who had been commandant at the Andersonville stockade.

His death was the ONE after the war, and many years later the United Daughters of the Confederacy in protest against his execution erected a memorial in his honor at Andersonville Prison Park.

Samuel John Mills Andrews was one of the many witnesses at that trial and hence he had obtained one of the transcripts which later became the booklet published in 1870.

After his ordeal and return home, Andrews married Louisa B. Reynolds who had been born in Cleveland, Ohio. Apparently for a year or two, the couple lived in Kansas, as their oldest child George R. was born there.

By 1870 Andrews and his family were again in Illinois, this time living in Clay County near Iola where he operated as a farmer. He wrote an introduction and had the transcript printed in Effingham, Illinois, not far from where he lived.

Andrews and his wife had other children: Mary E., John W., Frankie and Arthur. Samuel John Mills Andrews died 2 February, 1897 at the age of 60 years 10 months and 10 days. His widow and children apparently moved as no record remained of them in Clay County, Illinois. Andrews' widow lived until 9 July, 1924, her death occurring at Elgin, Kane County, Illinois. Both Samuel and Louisa Andrews were buried next to their child Frankie in Keen's Chapel Cemetery, Clay County, Illinois.

TAKEN IN.

SUFFERINGS

OF

UNION SOLDIERS

IN

SOUTHERN PRISONS.

BY SAMUEL J. M. ANDREWS,
A Disabled Soldier of the 17th Regiment Ill. Infantry, who was a
Prisoner for more than a year in the South.

REGISTER PRINT, EFFINGHAM, ILL.
1870.

NARRATIVE.

When the astounding though not unlooked-for intelligence came that the first gun had been fired; that the conflict was indeed begun, and that Fort Sumter had fallen and was in the hands of traitors, then was demonstrated the safety of our national policy—dependence on its citizen soldiery. The mother's joy, the father's hope, the sister's pride, sprang to arms with an alacrity heretofore unparalleled in history, and rushed forth willingly—nay, with proud joy at the privilege of being counted worthy to do battle in so noble a cause.

The privations of camp life, the weary march, the performance of the dangerous picket duty—aye, even the dreadful realities of the battle field, were counted as nothing compared with the honor of upholding our insulted flag. These were counted in the cost. But, it was not looked for, or expected, that those, who, through the fortunes of war, fell into

the hands of the enemy, should by them be thrust
into dismal, filthy dungeons, and allowed to be de-
voured by vermin, or rot or starve, till death was
welcome, or be turned into an open field in mid-
winter, with no other shelter save the blue arch of
heaven, and not wood enough to cook the corn-cob
meal and putrid meat, to say nothing of enough to
warm their freezing frames; having previously been
robbed of all, save barely sufficient to cover nakedness, and not always even that. The question has
been asked a thousand times, and is still asked, if
the stories which are told of the horrors of prison
life in the South are true? Alas, they are too true!

We have read of the sufferings of the Christian
martyrs in the dark ages. We have read of the in-
quisition, of the tortures of the rack; but all these
fade into insignificance when compared to the terri-
ble, hellish atrocities which have been perpetrated
on Union soldiers in this nineteenth century, and
that, too, by their own brothers. Language fails to
describe—imagination to picture the reality. I
speak what I know, have seen, and have myself suffered. You ask, how did any live? I answer, few
did, as more than sixty thousand graves of Union
soldiers, starved to death at Libby, Andersonville,
and other prison pens of the South, fully testify. I
have seen fellow-soldiers in mid-winter, with but a
few rotten rags, insufficient to hide their fleshless
bones, living, staggering skeletons, reduced to idiocy,
and looking to the grave as a happy release.

I have seen my comrades lashed to the stake, and subjected to the humiliating agony of a hundred lashes with a "cat-o'-nine-tails," merely for the gratification of this same chivalry.

I have seen fellow-soldiers that were torn in pieces by hounds for doing that which, by all civilized nations, is counted an honor—attempting to escape; and I have seen another suspended by the thumbs for hours for the same offence. This took place at Florence, South Carolina. The excruciating agony which this man endured beggars all description.

I have seen hundreds vaccinated with diseased virus, from which the most filthy, loathesome and painful sores were the result; from which the necessity of amputation was almost certain; and from which again death was equally certain. And this virus infused into the system an hereditary disease which, should the unfortunate wretch escape death, is transmissible to posterity.

Was a parallel ever known? The records of savage barbarity and torture are outdone in comparison.

At one time, not a morsel of food of any kind was issued to us for three days. This withholding prisoners' rations for three consecutive days was universal throughout the so-called Confederacy. We had often been without for one or two days, but this time we were without for three days together, during which time recruiting officers came among us with the comforting assurance that our government cared nothing for us and would not exchange. A few were weak enough to yield to their arguments and enlist with them to save their lives, as they thought; but they did the rebs little good, for the first time they got a chance, they run away into our own lines, and those that did not succeed in escaping, were sent back to prison.

Those three days of woe and anguish will never be forgotten until the last of those sufferers lies silent in the grave.

Oh, with what brutal satisfaction and delight did the brave commander kick and beat the helpless wretches who, driven by hunger, dared to ask for food.

Andersonville was a treble stockade, enclosing twenty-five acres of ground with no shelter whatever provided for the thirty thousand men who were there confined. We were compelled to endure alike the scorching heat of summer and the bitter blasts of winter.

For twenty-two successive days the pelting storm beat upon our devoted heads. Oh, who shall tell the suffering endured in those three long weeks? What scenes of horror were witnessed there! At morning dawn, look which way you might, the emaciated, haggard forms of comrades whom death had released from their sufferings, met the aching gaze of the heart-sick survivor who would himself gladly exchange places with them.

As the sun rose high in heaven, all around were to

be seen the half-naked, blistering forms of fellow-be-
ings stretched on the scorching sand, while from their
yet living bodies were issuing loathesome maggots
with which the ground was completely covered, making it impossible to move without treading on them.
I draw no picture from fancy—I speak the plain,
unvarnished truth.

Here men were confined in the stocks, exposed to
the broiling heat of the sun for days, while no comrade dared show pity or give relief, even a drop of
water to cool their raging thirst, on pain of being
himself incarcerated.

I have seen these poor starving beings go to the
sinks, and from out the filth there gather and eat the
scraps which the more fortunate ones had cast away,
while others picked up the undigested food which
weaker stomachs were unable to retain.

In all promiscuous assemblies of men there are
those who need only to be cut loose from the re-
strainst of civilized society and of law and order, to allow them to descend to the lowest level which it is
possible for human depravity to reach. Nor did we
find an exception to this rule among our fellow prisoners. If we would look for sympathy to exist any-
where we should look for it among companions in
misery. But our cup of sorrow was not yet full—as
if it was not enough to be abused, robbed and mur-
dered by our enemies, there must needs be those among
ourselves whose base treachery could impel them to
rob the few who had successfully eluded the greedy

rapacity of their captors, getting inside with a few
cents or some little article of real or attributed value,
which might be traded to the rebel for a pint of
meal or beans, and then imbrue their hands in the gore
of their hapless victims.

But this state of things could not last—the mass
arose against it. A vigilance committee was institut-
ed. A police force was organized. A court of justice
was convened and six of these villains paid the penalty
of their crimes on the scaffold. These men were, by
their comrade-prisoners, regularly tried, as highwaymen and murderers, in the first degree, found guilty,
and executed within the stockade, at Andersonville,
July 11, 1864.

Then followed a reaction. The police finding
themselves invested with almost unlimited power, began to abuse the confidence which had been placed in
them, until the name of "policeman" became a terror,
many making use of their temporary power to revenge
private quarrels.

I must notice our prison guard, and as another has
described them, I prefer making the quotation from
him :

"They, as a general rule, with some isolated exceptions, were the most ignorant class of men I have ever
seen and brutish in proportion. There was occasionally a conscript among them who was kind, but always wishing the war was over.

"Occasionally a gentleman was found among these
guards, and officers disposed to kindness, but the great

mass were ignorant scoundrels, who would sell sand to our starving men for meal, taking special care to have the money handed through the hole in the stockade to them before they handed in the supposed wallet of meal to the purchaser, and all trade being in violation of orders, no complaint could be filed with the officers.

"On one or more occasions the guards would call a Yank up to the stockade to trade with him, while another guard would shoot him for crossing the dead line, and for this brave act of chivalry would obtain a thirty day furlough.

"I knew of one case even worse than this. After a party of Union soldiers had been captured thirty-six hours, and disarmed, five of them were shot dead on the spot, the sixth being shot in the right corner of the right eye, passing out near the right ear. This man feigned to be dead for several hours, and by this means saved his life.

"As to these guards, both the cradle and the grave were robbed. Boys from twelve to fifteen years of age, and old men from forty to eighty, made up this strange and motly crew, and most of them State militia, who had never seen the elephant, that is, had never been to the front.

"Only those who have been prisoners themselves, and those who have been to the front, know how to treat prisoners. These gentlemen and the butter-milk cavalry are extremely brave and despotic when in possession of an unarmed Yank."

These facts and observations I can fully corrobo-
rate from my own personal experience.

I cannot pass the prison hospital without notice,
for there were places connected with these great Gol-
gothas which were called hospitals ; but what shall
I call them ?—slaughter pens? Even that name is
inadequate. Here the fact of the brutality with
which men can treat their comrades in suffering was
practically demonstrated. Here were to be found
men—our men—nurses, who could not only see their
companions suffer for the want of the little atten-
tions which might have been given them here, but
could actually abuse them while life did last, and
then fight over the rags they left.

These were the very individuals whom the rebs,
facetious in their kindness, selected for nurses. Occasionally a kind-hearted man would, through the
influence of some of the more kindly disposed sur-
geons, get the privilege of taking care of some of
them, but such instances were few and far between.

I will relate a circumstance: I was myself a pa-
tient in the hospital, from a wound received when
captured. Our nurse was one of these brutes. There
was one poor boy whom he seemed to delight in
abusing. By and by this nurse fell sick himself, and
it was necessary that some one should take his place,
which I got the privilege of doing, being convales-
cent. When I told the boys, this poor fellow, al-
though too weak to speak distinctly, clasped his
hands, and exclaimed with the little remaining

strength he had, "I'm so glad, I'm so glad, I'm so glad." I am proud to feel that it was in my power to make his last hours less bitter than they otherwise would have been.

Oh, the horrors of this place! Would that I might pass it by without notice; but truth, justice and humanity demand that it should be published to the world.

Here were crowded together the miserable victims of exposure, disease and starvation, until, if from no other cause, the very malaria of the atmosphere would make a well man sick.

And these men were fed with what was called bread, made from the siftings of corn meal, not unfrequently ground with the cob in it.

Here, too, were gathered the miserable victims of the vaccination before mentioned, and the wounded taken in battle.

Here the young surgical bloods amused themselves with cutting off, by hundreds, limbs, which they sagely pronounced needed to be amputated to save life ; and what opposition could the helpless victims make ?

The actual number of deaths was astounding. For awhile, during the month of August, '64, the number per day was a hundred and forty. Of this fact I had an opportunity to know, for I was in the hospital whither all the bodies were brought before—shall I say burial?—buried as a barbarian would scorn to bury his dog.

Oh, the revolting scenes which we were daily compelled to witness ; the emaciated and mutilated forms of our beloved brothers and comrades, with brutal jest tumbled into an ox cart and drawn off to the "potter's field," where they were thrown into a trench and covered with the clods of the valley, without even a blanket for a winding sheet.

But the darkest night must have an end, and the time came at last when the prison gates were opened —a few of us lived to see it—but oh, who shall tell of our condition ?   When we arrived in our lines, the general, and officers and men who received us—men of iron, men who had faced the roaring cannon and breasted its iron hail, and witnessed the carnage of the battle-field unmoved, men who for years had not known a tear, were overwhelmed and wept like babes when they saw us unclothed, unfed, freezing, haggard, staggering skeletons, clinging to each other for support, as we tottered across the neutral ground.

And when we again caught sight of the stars and stripes—that glorious flag for which we had suffered so much, and which was now once more proudly floating over us—Oh, great God, thou alone can tell the thrill which vibrated through our helpless frames. For some, already tottering on the brink of the grave, the sight was too much—the joy was too great ; and they yielded up their lives at the very moment of the realization of their fondest hopes—died, when fruition was just within their grasp.

Shall I tell of our receptions ?   Each vied with the

other. None could do enough. Wherever we went, the best was set before us. We had not even to speak, for our utmost wishes and wants were anticipated, till we were repaid for all our suffering, by the universal welcome and the open and outstretched arms with which we were received.

"I must close my hurried account. It is far from being full. Not half has been told. By far the most has been kept back, from very shame, and out of respect for the reader. I have not embellished this narrative. The pictures were too rough, the characters too forlorn for the flowers of rhetoric to bloom in their presence. Broken hearts, crushed spirits, and manhood trampled on, may answer as fitting subjects for the romancer's pen, but the horrible reality, so seldom seen, burns its images upon the beholder's soul, that no other impressions can efface, and they remain life-pictures indeed."

And these men were young and noble and brave, who suffered these things, guilty of no crime but that their loved their country's flag and would not forsake it.

Suffering so vast in its extent, so fearful in its results, no history records, no pen can describe, no pencil paint.

I once thought, as you perhaps to-day think, that these stories could not be true; that it was not in the heart of human beings to treat each other as we were told that southern soldiers treated northern ones. Fiends might do these things, but men were not dev-

ils, and anything that fell below these could not prac-
tice the systematic, sickening barbarities which' we
daily read and heard that our own countrymen perpetrated on each other. But I am cured of my skepti-
cism; for I have seen my comrades, my own countrymen, in my own land, in this nineteenth century, ab-
solutely frozen, tortured, starved to death.

Incredible as it may seem, the awful horrors of
Libby, of Andersonville, of Florence, of Saulsbury,
are facts. Some seized at the faintest shadow of an
excuse for such suffering, and when it was said that
we were fed as well as their own soldiers, it was hop-
ed this might in some degree palliate their treatment
of our men. But the course of our victorious armies
through their fruitful fields, has settled all doubts
on this point.

When we were captured and were being taken to
prison, they exultantly showed us their well filled
barns and tauntingly asked what we thought of starving them out, defiantly boasting that they had provisions for twenty years. Neither before God nor
man has the South the faintest shadow of excuse for
dooming her prisoners of war to slow death by freez
ing, starvation or cruelty.

Northern people say that Jefferson Davis was not
a bad-hearted man. Did he know that in his domin-
ions stood, with their burdens of sin and suffering,
these prison walls of agony, crying unto God? Was
it by his consent and authority these things were
done?

Northern men and women praise Gen. Robert E. Lee, for a courteous and kind-hearted gentleman. Did he ever, by word or stroke of his pen, oppose or alleviate the sufferings that for all these years had been going on under his eyes?

Where were the wives of these men, that they did not, with tears and supplications, give their husbands no rest till they prevailed upon them to relieve the awful miseries that were going on by day and night among their prisoners of war? Is it not woman's place and duty to be pitiful or sympathetic when man is full of revenge and cruelty? Take the vilest crowd of criminals that were ever herded together beneath one prison roof, and tell to any woman throughout the whole North the half of such a story of horror as we have been told, of husbands, and sons and brothers, and if that woman would not risk her own life to carry food, clothing, and medicine to those men, she would be unworthy her name and sex.

We all know that magnanimity and generosity become conquerors—that courtesy and clemency are the part of victors towards the vanquished, and that the first duty of a Christian nation is to set an example of forbearance and forgiveness; but because of this, shall we open to them the doors of our asylums? Shall we smile upon and take into our confidence highwaymen and murderers? Shall the men who rattled into Lawrence with the early dawn, and slayed her helpless fathers, and sons, and brothers—shall the men who could see day by day the famishing eyes, the pinched faces, the skeleton forms of our starving men—shall they go altogether unpunished?

Does not a voice come up to us from those thousands of southern graves, where lie our heroic dead, crying for vengeance, demanding that at least for the cause of justice, truth and humanity, the names of the men who commanded and allowed, and those who executed these demoniac atrocities, shall be given to universal execration and infamy. Let them be a byword and reproach through all time. Let not their gray hairs come down to the grave in peace.

Talk of mercy! Did they show us, their helpless victims, mercy? Would they have been lenient, had they succeeded?

Oh, what an inestimable triumph have we achieved, by showing to the world that this government can and will be sustained. Let us not fail, each day, to render our profoundest gratitude to our Universal Sovereign for a Union inseparable.

Comrades, who have suffered in Confederate hells, we have been companions in bitter wo, where all around was only the blackness of darkness, where no ray of light shone into the dark, dark future. But we have yet the proud consciousness that we never forsook our country's flag.

We now meet as men—as freemen—as the champions of Liberty. And when, in years to come, we meet, the name of Libby, of Andersonville, or any of those prison-pens, will be a watch-word which shall open wide the doors of hospitality else unknown.

THE REBEL PRISON.

[SELECTED AND REVISED.]

Comrades who have lived, once more
    Our dear old flag to view,
Rejoice, and let our hearts be glad,
    As they ever have been true.
We've bid adieu to corn-cob bread,
    Bid adieu to putrid meat,
And by friends once more are welcomed
    To our old long-vacant seat.

Welcomed by friends, ever mindful
    Of the absent loved one dear,
As oft again rolled down the cheek,
    An unbidden tell-tale tear;
And as around the well filled board,
    At evening they would come,
When the labors and the toils,
    Of the weary day were done,

Then asked the mother "where's my boy?"
    Dreamed the wife with tearful eye,
Her husband in a dungeon lay,
    Starving, praying he might die;
But oh, they knew not of our woes,
    And no one can ever tell,
But only they who have been in
    The dark, dismal prison cell!

How often, as we set around
    Our little smoky blaze,
We'd hear some youthful comrade speak,
    In some gentle sweetheart's praise,
Or we'd hear as young a comrade
    Tell about a loving bride,
He had wed since war's beginning,
    And for whom he would have died.

Some of us have little notions;
    Oft we'd sit, day after day,
Cutting bones, all shapes and sizes,
    Just to while the hours away.
Things of grotesque shape possesing,
    Some to cherished friends we bring,
And they'll keep them as momentoes,
    Yes, they'll cherish everything.

And they'll tell how that we made them,
    To make time the shorter seem;
Tell how while we were making,
    Still we of our homes did dream.
They will deem them neatly finished,
    Keep them till the future, for
Could they speak, they'd often tell you
    Of some sufferer of war.

There are three days we'll ne'er forget,
    Till the storms of life are passed,
For in those three days of anguish,
    None in prison broke his fast;
For there were no rations brought us,
    Even of the corn-cob bread,
Oh, we tell the truth of prison,
    Yet the truth cannot be said.

Dear friends, when storms wo'd gather dark,
    Then we'd think of homes afar,
Homes where there was warmth and shelter,
    Notwithstanding frowns of war;

But in those bristling prisons bare,
    We'd to brave the trying storms,
While we were shivering in our rags,
    Scarce enough to hide our forms.

Yonder sky our umberella,
    And the only one we had,
Think of that, and never wonder,
    That the prisoner's heart was sad ;
Think of that, and never wonder
    That so many had to die,
That so many hearts lie silent,
    'Neath that far off prison sky.

But now our prison lives are o'er,
    Oh, it is a pleasant thought,
Dear loved and cherished friends, by whom
    We have never been forgot ;
And as again, we find us in
    Our old familiar chairs,
Your smiles of welcome half repay
    Us, for all our griefs and cares.

A P P E N D I X.

———•———

AN EPITOME OF THE TESTIMONY

GIVEN AT THE

W I R Z   T R I A L.

———•———

[Capt. Henry Wirtz, the Confederate officer in immediate command of the prison stockade at Andersonville, was, in the year 1865, tried by a Military Commission, at Washington, D.C., and convicted and executed for his brutality to the prisoners under his control.]

———•———

FEDERAL TESTIMONY.

Andrew J. Spring, sworn—Was in a Connecticut regiment; was captured, and went to Andersonville prison on the 3d of May, 1864, and was put into the stockade on the 27th of May, 1864; was assigned to duty in the cook-house. The meal consisted of the

corn and cob ground together, and baked without
salt two-thirds of the time. Bacon was frequently
brought in in quarters, and was frequently full of
maggots before it was cooked. It was frequently issued raw in the stockade; issued no vegetables, al-
though there were plenty of vegetables in the vicin-
ity. Witness smuggled vegetables to the prisoners
which he procured of men of the 55th Georgia regiment. A rebel surgeon, named Selman, was sutler
inside the stockade, until he got all the boys' greenbacks. There was plenty of green corn; there were
from seventy-five to one hundred acres of corn near
the Fifty-Fifth Georgia regiment. Orders were issued by Captain Wirz, prohibiting the rebels trading
with Union prisoners. Wirz confiscated all the fruit
and vegetables he could which the prisoners would
get. He promised the guard half the peaches they
would confiscate, as they came to the gate of the
stockade. Witness bribed the lieutenant at the gate
with twelve dollars to get in and spend an hour with
his comrades. Witness could not recognize many of
his own men, they had become so lean. Saw many
in the stockade who had become idiots; they wan-
dered about, not knowing where they were going;
saw some lying apparently dead. Witness knew 8
or 10 who applied for fatigue duty. They went out
and were returning with wood, when they stopped
to rest. Captain Wirz rode by, when one of them
asked him for an extra ration. He replied as he
commonly did, in opprobrious and indecent language,

that he would put every Yankee in the stocks and
starve them to death. To a man who had escaped,
he used even worse language, saying he would shoot
him if he ever attempted to escape again, as sure as
he (Wirz) was going to hell, and he knew he was going there. These were his usual remarks. Witness
saw from five hundred to one thousand acres of tim-
ber when he went there, but it was all cut down so as
to use the artillery, as they expected a raid from
Stoneman to release the prisoners. Saw Wirz, Turner
and others bring in a prisoner about the last of August, or the first of September, bitten badly by the
dogs. One of the men said they shook him out of a
tree. Saw thirteen in a chain-gang at one time in
two ranks. They had a chain and shackle to each
ankle ; could step about eight inches and had to keep
step. Also had a sixty-four pound ball to every four
men, and a small ball and chain to the outside feet.—
A chain was fastened around their necks, bringing
them in a circle. They were put in for attempting
to escape. I saw a man shot by the sentry. Capt.
Wirz was on the sentry-box when he was shot. He
came into the stockade and drew his revolver, saying
he would shoot the men if they did not disperse. I
saw another shot while asleep under his blanket. He
had rolled under the dead-line. I saw our negroes,
prisoners of war, taken out and receive fifty or seventy-five lashes because they refused to work on account
of being sick. A man named Humes whipped them.

There were a class of boys from ten to fifteen years

old, and men from forty to seventy, who took a pride
in shooting our men whenever they were put on as
sentries.

There were good Union men in the Fifty-fifth
Georgia.

All of the chain-gang had to lie down, whenever
one lay down. I saw men in chains for two months.

J. E. Alden, being sworn, testified that he had
been orderly sergeant of Co. F, Fourth Vermont regiment; was in Andersonville; arrived there on the
12th of July; were taken to Wirz' head-quarters,
counted off in squads, and put in the stockade. Some
of the men were naked and terribly emaciated. The
supply of wood was very bad; had seen men digging
for roots in the swamp which was filled with maggots
from fifteen to twenty inches deep. Nearly every
morning dead men were found on the bank of the
creek, without clothing. These were men who died
from starvation. Witness, after roll call, would have
all the sick go to the south gate for sick call. Four
or five thousand would sometimes crowd about the
gate, which was very small. Had seen men crawl
up to the doctor on their hands and knees, and plead
for medicines, or to be taken to the hospital. The
doctors would often order them to be taken back to
the stockade, saying they could live until the next
morning. Had been in the hospital for two or three
months as nurse; the sick were treated very bad in
the hospital; they had to lay on the ground with lit-

tle or no clothing or blankets, and the food was very bad. In June there were twenty-four rainy days; about two hundred sick were lying out without shelter. Wirz took command about the last of March or first of April. The first day he said he had to muster and count us all, and unless he got through by 2 o'clock, the prisoners should have no rations that day. He did not get through, and the prisoners were kept without rations that day. A man named Stevenson died; he had respectable clothes on; witness requested Captain Wirz to let the clothes remain on the body; he said he would. Wirz, with two soldiers, (rebels,) went out and took the clothes from the man and buried him naked. I saw a man whose throat had been torn to pieces by the dogs. His clothes were all torn off, and the marks of the dogs could be seen. Captain Wirz, Dr. White and Stevenson were there at the time. Wirz said, " It serves the dog right." The man died the same day. A friend of witness was lying on the ground nearly dead with the diarrhoea, and he could not go down to the sink. The sick man asked the Captain to give him a piece of bread, as he could not go for his rations, whereupon the Captain struck him over the head with his riding whip, and the man swooned. He was taken to the hospital and died shortly after. I knew a man who was lying in the stocks senseless. Out of the seventy-one men captured with witness, about twelve were living now.

I saw two or three men reaching over the dead-line

for water. Heard the Captain tell the sentry to shoot them. The sentinel fired and killed one man. I renognized Captain Wirz, and heard his voice when he ordered the sentry. The Captain told the sentry if a man had his arm over the dead line he must shoot him, or he would have him punished. I saw the man called Chickamauga shot. Wirz ordered the sentry to shoot the man. The sentry fired and killed him.

The were about one dozen beds in the hospital in the month of June. That was before the hospital was enlarged. I was in the hospital until the latter part of August. About seventy-five to one hundred prisoners were in a ward. A ward would accommodate about fifty or sixty men comfortably. At one time about two hundred were lying outside without any shelter. Dr. White was in charge of them. They were made of canvas tents, which were very bad. During rain, the ground would be wet and muddy. At the time I saw the man who had been torn by the dogs, I heard the Captain say, it served him right, and he " wouldn't care if all the Yankees in the stockade were served the same way."

Wm. H. Jennings, (colored,) sworn—Had been in the 8th United States colored infantry ; was taken to Andersonville; was there about one year. About one month after witness was put in the stockade he was put to work digging a ditch; witness had been wounded in the thigh, and the wound was bleeding, and painful. I had been whipped by order of Captain Wirz; had received thirty lashes because I was not able to go to work; was whipped on the bare skin, and then put in the stocks and kept there a day and night without anything to eat or drink. Had seen a man who was torn by the hounds, who died shortly afterwards. Had seen men who had lost their arms from vaccination. I never had my wounds dressed; was compelled to work by the Captain. The man who whipped me said it was done by Wirz's orders.

Thomas N. Way, being sworn, testified that he had been in the United States service in an Ohio regiment. He was a prisoner at Andersonville, and knew Captain Wirz. He put him in the stocks for eight days. He tied him up by the thumbs for fifteen minutes because he was not able to stand up in the ranks. Could not use his hands for two months after he was tied up by the thumbs. At the time witness made his escape and was recaptured, Wirz said he should be put in the stocks four days. At the end of four days, he was taken out. The Captain told four men to take him to the stockade, when witness said jestingly, " I am much obliged to you, Captain, for having me carried. I am not able to walk." Wirz said, "I puts you in the stocks four days more, and if you gives me any more lip, I will shoot you." Witness was then taken back and put in the stocks, and had to lay there with his face to the sun. Knew a young prisoner 17 years old who was caught by the dogs and torn to

pieces. He died immediately. This witness had
been caught by the dogs three times. Heard the
Captain give orders to shoot men: had been bucked
and gagged because he was late at roll call: had seen
many prisoners punished in that way: was told by
the guards when men were shot, that they were ordered to do so by Captain Wirz. This witness described his experience with the ball and chain, which
was put on him for trying to escape. At first five
men were chained by one foot to a large ball, a small
ball being attached to the other foot. The number
was increased, and four men were hitched to a large
ball, each with a small ball attached to the other
foot, and they were formed into a chain gang by putting iron collars upon their necks attached to each
other by chains two feet long: was confined in this
manner twenty-five days, being liberated one hour out
of every five hours.

The first punishment inflicted on him was some-
time in July. The next act was being tied up by the
thumbs, a day or two afterwards: the next was the
ball and chain, which was kept on him twenty-five
days: was in the stocks four days at each time. The
punishments were inflicted for trying to get away.—
This witness knew of the attempt to tunnel out and
turn the guns on the guards: was not concerned in
it: witness had been chased by the hounds.

[This witness was here taken sick on the stand, and
had to retire from the court-room.]

John H. Stearns, being duly sworn, testified that he had been in the United States service : was in the hospital as steward. Saw one man brought into the hospital shot through the breast, and powder was in the wound, showing that the musket was near him when fired. The man afterwards died. Saw four others who received gunshot wounds in the stockade. Had seen from eight to twelve men in the chain-gang : saw them almost daily : saw one man in the gang who was very feeble, and hardly able to walk. Afterwards heard he died. The men brought from the hospital to the stocks were nearly naked. This witness remembered one case where the maggots were covering a man. They attacked his eyes, nose and ears : had penetrated the rectum, causing excruciating pain. In three or four hours he died. Very many of the cases brought to the hospital from the stockade were delirious ; had seen several men covered with maggots. Knew one man who was shot near the hospital by a sentry ; the limb was amputated, and the man died the next day. The patients who had limbs amputated most always died. Had seen men who had been vaccinated ; the vaccine matter seemed to produce a syphilitic sore, such as is produced by the disease itself. Heard Wirz cursing a prisoner, and telling him if he did not get up he would shoot him. There were no beds in the hospital ; some few bunks were there ; on one occasion witness asked for poles and brush to make beds ; Wirz refused him, saying he would put him in the stockade.

Wm. Willis Scott, being sworn, testified that he belonged to the 6th West Virginia cavalry, and was captured on the 26th of June, 1864, and arrived at Andersonville about the middle of August, 1864. On the 26th or 27th of August, a sick man was sitting on the bank near the gate of the stockade. Wirz came along, and the man asked the Captain if he could get up. The Captain took out his revolver and beat him over the head and shoulders with the butt end of it.

L. S. Pond, being sworn, testified that he belonged to the 2d New York heavy artillery; went into Andersonville prison on June 28th, 1861, and was there nearly four months. On arriving, Captain Wirz ordered the Union sergeant to count them off into squads of ninety men each ; he then ordered his own officers to search them. Blankets, etc., were taken away from them. One man from Michigan had taken from him, by Wirz, a daguerreotype likeness of his wife and two children. The man asked that it be returned, when the Captain threw it on the ground and crushed it with his feet ; witness afterward learned that the likeness was that of the dead wife of the prisoner and his children. There was also taken from another prisoner a likeness of his young lady, concerning which the officers under the Captain made some very vulgar remarks, and then carried the likeness away with them. Before going, the young man asked for it, and a pistol was placed to his head with

a threat to blow out his brains.   In the latter part of
July, 1864, a man reached for water under the dead-
line, when he was shot by a guard, who said, " There
goes for a ten day's furlough."   The man who was
shot was taken out of the stream by his comrades.
This witness saw men who were wounded in the arms
and legs by dogs.   The men had tried to escape.
Only three sticks of cord-wood were brought into the
prison to cook the rations of 270 men for two days.
Witness always bade his comrades good-bye when
they were taken into the hospital, as he never expected to see them again.

Rufus Mundy, being sworn, testified that he belonged to the 75th Ohio; was captured on the 26th
of June, 1862, and arrived at Andersonville on the
3rd day of February, 1865.   About the 21st of February, 1865, the prisoners had borrowed a number
of spades and shovels, and on the next morning one
was missing.   Capt. Wirz ordered the men in line,
when one man who was sick did not get in line.   The
Captain picked up a piece of brick and struck the man
near the ear, which knocked him over.   On the 10th
of March, of the same year, when the men were hauled up, a sick man stood up an hour, and then sat
down.   The Captain ordered him to fall in, but he
did not hear it.   The Captain then walked up to him
and kicked him, and when the prisoner regained his
feet, his mouth or nose was bleeding.

Abner A. Kelley, being sworn, testified that he belonged to the 40th New Hampshire. He arrived at Andersonville and was taken to head-quarters, where Captain Wirz had them counted off in squads of ninety each, after which, blankets, canteens, and pocket-books were taken from them, and then carried into the Captain's office. In August, 1864, a sick man laid at the stockade gate, with a sore on his back as large as a man's hand, and the maggots were in the sore. A sergeant asked the Captain to let him be carried out for treatment. The Captain refused, saying, "Let him lay there and die." The man did die.

Sidney Smith, being sworn, testified that he belonged to the 14th Connecticut. He was taken prisoner and carried to Andersonville. Saw Wirz knock down a prisoner outside the stockade with his revolver. This witness heard the guard say when they shot a Union prisoner they got thirty days' furlough. Heard Witz tell a guard to bayonet a sick man.

——— Brunner, being sworn, testified that he belonged to the 14th Connecticut; was captured and arrived at Andersonville on the 22d of February, 1864. One morning, Wirz missed a man in the stockade, and gave the prisoners no rations until he was found. In March, 1864, this witness was sick. Wirz came to his tent with a revolver in his hand, and said he would kill him. Witness replied, " I

would be better off then." Wirz then threw him out
of the tent and kicked him.

Thomas H. Howe, 102d New York, being sworn,
testified, that he went to Andersonville on the 29th
of July, 1864, and saw Wirz on that day. He said
he was going to search the prisoners, and if they did
not keep still he was going to shoot them. Watches,
money, canteens and blankets were taken away from
the prisoners. A knife and fork were taken away
from the witness. Two ten dollar notes he saved by
putting them in his mouth. Saw $100 taken from a
young man near him. The effects taken were all
turned over to Wirz. This witness could not without difficulty find room to lie down in the stockade;
and when he did lie down, he could not sleep because
of the suffering and groaning everywhere around him.
The men there were mere skeletons, and many of
them were very crazy. In October, 1864, a crazy
man went over the dead line and was shot. Another
went over afterwards, but the men got him back;
witness saw men shot who had not reached the dead-
line; Wirz was present at the time; the rations were
stopped three days in August, because the sick men
could not get to roll-call. They were stopped two
days in September for the same reason.

Major General J. H. Wilson, being sworn, testified
that he had examined the stockade. It could have
been better located about 250 feet from the hospital.

There was a large creek fifteen feet wide and five feet deep, which would have given an ample supply of water for the men, while the stream through the stockade would not supply over four or five thousand.

John H. Fisher, colored, being duly sworn, testified, that he had belonged to the 8th United States colored troops. On the first of October he was bucked and gagged at Andersonville. The man who did it said it was done by order of Captain Wirz. He saw the Captain draw a pistol on a man named George Brown, and he told him if he did not run he would shoot him. Two colored men were whipped at the grave-yard because they refused to work. Saw the marks of the lash; the blood had been drawn. This witness refused to work because he was bare-footed and naked. He was bucked and gagged when he was whipped. He received thirty-nine lashes. Saw three men whipped; they had marks of the strap; the strap was two and a half feet long, and as broad as witness' three fingers.

Henry Lull, being sworn, testified that he had belonged to the 146th New York. He arrived at Andersonville on the 22d of May, 4864, and left there on the eleventh day of September of the same year. The rations were stopped three days at one time, because some of the prisoners were absent at roll-call. Some one there made a complaint to Wirz at headquarters that they had not enough bread to keep them, when Wirz said he had enough bread to keep them twenty years. This witness saw a man whipped for refusing to work; he received fifty lashes; he also saw three men shot, and saw upwards of fifteen after they had been shot. The name of one who was shot was Hawe, of a western regiment; he was shot on the 18th of August in the stockade, about ten yards inside of the dead-line; he was shot by   ᵔᵔntinel. Saw the first one shot on the 28th of M..y ᵕ the east side of the stockade; he accidentally stepped on the dead-line in trying to avoid a mud-hole. The shot took effect in his hip: the third man witness saw shot was in the middle of July, when he was reaching for water: he was shot in the breast and died on the spot.

Felix de la Baum, being sworn, testified that he was in the 79th New York; was at Andersonville. On the 8th day of July he was not allowed to go the water. Had seen men tied up by the thumbs; had seen Capt. Wirz shoot twice at men. One man he saw was wounded in the breast. He was shot by Wirz with a revolver. This witness had seen men fall down in fits who had no water in twenty-four hours. They at one time had the guard tied up by the thumbs for two hours for giving a prisoner some trifling liberty. The man who was shot by Wirz in the breast died shortly afterwards. In December, 1864, Captain Wirz allowed squads of twenty-five each to gather wood; witness and his comrade hid

10

themselves when they heard the dogs bark; the dogs
came up and bit his comrade, and they were captured
by those in charge of the dogs.   Had seen men with
ball and chain.   One man was crazy from starvation,
and said he was Samson, and was chained to try his
strength.   This witness had seen men shot on the
dead-line; had seen men bucked and gagged.   This
witness was robbed of everything he had, even his
clothes.   Those who had wood could buy enough
wood for a one-dollar greenback to cook a cup of
coffee.   When he was captured he weighed 455
pounds, and when he arrived at Hilton Head he
weighed but 98 pounds.   The bacon at times was all
rotten.   He had been wounded; he asked Wirz for
a bandage to dress his leg. Wirz asked him his name,
and, with an oath (calling witness a Frenchman),
"What did you want to fight us for?" This witness
had to be carried into the stockade on several occasions, on account of weakness.

Father Hamilton, a Roman Catholic clergyman,
testified that he resided at Macon, Georgia; was
called to Andersonville in February, 1865.   There
was a great deal of sickness and starvation there at
the time.   The stockade was alive with vermin.   The
witness said that in the performance of his duty he
had occasion to take off his coat, and in less than than
five minutes it was covered with filth and alive with
vermin.   In the latter part of May he heard of an el-
derly man by the name of Farrell shot at the dead-

line.   Witness said that the hospital was very crowded, and nearly all were afflicted with the scurvy and diarrhoea.   The accommodations were scant and the prisoners had no beds.   There was no shelter.   He could not see any tents and but few blankets.   The heat in the hospital was intense.   There were sawmills near Andersonville.   He had administered the last consolation of religion to the dying at the rate of twenty-five to thirty per day.   Had seen men walk about the premises entirely nude.   This witness had administered sacrament to prisoners who were covered with vermin, and had to lie down alongside of them, as they were too far gone; had seen them with all sorts of sores, and covered with flies and maggots; had seen them dig in the earth to cover their bodies.

Charles E. Tibbles sworn.   Was in the 4th Iowa Infantry; was at Andersonville and escaped: saw Captain Wirz take a man by the throat and draw his pistol, threatening to shoot: witness was not allowed to go to the fire.   The rations, when he went there were two ounces of meat.   They were ordered to bury their own filth, and they buried it from one foot to eighteen inches deep, and after a rain it would be washed out of the trenches and scattered all over the camp again: and when the weather was warm, the filth would be turned into lice and maggots.   During his imprisonment, he was vaccinated, and his arm was very sore, so much so that he could not use it.   While in that condition he was branded by the

Doctor in charge, with caustic, on the back, with the initials, " U. S.," saying, "there, they will know you when they see you again."

Jasper Cullen, being sworn, testified that he belonged to the 1st Wisconsin, and arrived at Andersonville on the 10th of March, 1864. Captain Wirz and Selner were there. The Captain had the prisoners counted off, and then told them to remain in ranks until they were permitted to break ranks. The Captain and Selner went away, and the prisoners, after standing a long time, broke ranks, supposing that the Captain and Selner were done with them. Heard Wirz afterwards say that they should have no rations that day, as they had broken ranks without orders. He would teach them to keep in ranks when ordered to do so. Saw the Captain knock a man down, who appeared to be sick at the time: witness was taken out of the stockade and put into the bakery to load and unload meal, etc. Some of the meal was very coarse, and much of it was ground with the cob. Some of it was mouldy, and was thrown aside, generally. Some of the meal was good. Saw men in the chain-gang nearly every day for about a month : they had a ball and chain to their feet and iron plates around their necks : they were then attached to 100-pound balls. One man remained in the gang about a month who was very sick, and was a great annoyance to his comrades. Saw him after he was taken out of the gang, but the 32-pound ball was still at-

tached to him, and he still carried the iron plate on
his neck.   This man died in the guard-house some-
time in July, having the ball still attached, and the
iron plate still about his neck.   Witness saw them
taken off after his death.   Saw men in the stocks frequently ; their feet were fastened up from the ground
in such a way that they were compelled to lie with
their backs on the ground and their faces exposed to
the sun ; saw one man kept in this position all day ;
he had been engaged in hauling about the prison ; saw
a man shot near the gate in the stockade and inside
the dead line, by a sentry in whose box he saw Captain Wirz directly after the shot was fired.   Some of
the boys once remarked that they would sooner ex-
pose their lives at the front with Sherman, than to
remain in the stockade.   Wirz replied that he was
doing more for the Confederacy than the army were.
At the time Stoneman's men came into the depot,
they were stripped of nearly all they had ; they were
left bare-footed and bare-headed.

A. D. Blair, being sworn, testified that he had been
in the 22d New York volunteers ; was a prisoner at
Andersonville.   Captain Wirz was in command of
the prison there.   Had heard men ask Wirz for rations ; he replied with an oath, and said we would
get all the rations we deserved, and that would be
little.   Had seen Wirz at the gate when sick men
were being carried out.   If they did not move fast
enough to please him, he would push them down.   I

11

escaped and got about thirty miles from the stockade;
was recaptured and put in the stocks; was kept there
five or six hours; had heard the sentries say it was
the orders of Captain Wirz that they were to
receive thirty days' furlough for every Yankee devil
they killed. On one occasion a large crowd had gathered around the brook; witness reached over the
dead-line to get some water. The sentry fired at him
and the bullet passed near his head, striking two other
men, one of whom was mortally wounded in his tent.
Wirz planted a range of flags inside the stockade, and
gave the order that if a crowd of two hundred should
gather in any one spot beyond those flags he would
fire grape and canister upon them.

Charles H. Russell, being sworn, testified that he
belonged to Company E, 1st Wisconsin cavalry. He
arrived at Andersonville on the 27th of May, 1864;
was taken to Wirz's quarters. The captain told his
orderly to take everything that Yankee had. He
threatened to shoot witness because he spoke to him
about their bad bread. He had his pistol in his
hand, presented it to witness' head, and threatened
to shoot him. Saw the Captain go up to a sentry
and shake his hand, and call him a 'billy boy,' after
he had shot a man. The swamp was eighteen inches
or two feet deep with maggots. Men had to pass
through there frequently. Have seen men in there
digging roots. Wirz said he had been an orderly
sergeant in an Illinois regiment, and was under Sigel.

Bernard O'Hare, being sworn, testified that he belonged to Company A, 6th New York cavalry, and was a prisoner at Andersonville. Saw from 128 to 133 lying dead in the dead house at one time.

John Burns Walker, being sworn, testified that he belonged to Company G, 141st Pennsylvania infantry. He was a prisoner at Andersonville. On one occasion 500 sick men were in the sick enclosure; witness took one man to the hospital, and Surgeon Russell said: "Take him back; he will live till to-morrow." On the 4th of September, 1864, witness saw Morris Prinville, Co. H, 7th Indiana infantry, shot in the head by a sentinel. His brains were scattered around where he fell.

George O. Smith, being sworn, testified that he belonged to Co. K, 4th United States cavalry, and had been a prisoner at Andersonville. He saw four men shot: saw three men killed with one shot: they were shot by the sentinel on post: saw another man shot while attempting to pick up some pieces of bread; heard Wirz tell the sentinel to fire at a man who was reaching under the dead-line for water. Wirz told him if he did not shoot those Yankees he would shoot him down. Heard Wirz order that men should be vaccinated: had seen men vaccinated: the flesh all rotted away, and many lost their arms. This witness was vaccinated, but washed his arm, and sucked the blood out so it would not take. One man refused to be vaccinated, and he was taken out and a ball and chain put on him: had seen men on the banks of the swamp picking up beans that had passed through men. They would wash and eat them.

Ambrose Henshaw, being sworn, testified that he belonged to the 4th United States cavalry, and was in Andersonville in 1864 : say one prisoner shot on the 6th or 7th of May, 1864; he was an idiot and reached over the dead-line for bread: saw a man who was called by some Chickamauga, and by others Pretty Polly, shot at the stockade gate in the last of May. Pretty Polly had asked the captain's leave to pass out, which was refused, and the captain ordered the sentinel to shoot him. This the sentinel was slow in doing, and the captain went up into the box with his revolver drawn, to shoot the sentinel, but the sentinel fired and killed the man. This witness asked the captain to allow him to remove the body of the deceased, when the captain replied, "take him and go to hell with him." The captain then ordered the sentinel to fire into a crowd of prisoners who had congregated to see who had been shot.

Thomas Walsh, being sworn, testified that he belonged to the 74th New York : read from a memorandum he made in his testament while in prison, as follows :

"March 26, no rations. March 27, no rations issued until 3 p. m. April 1, no rations. April 2, is-

sued at 5 P. M.—mule flesh and a pint of meal; April
8, Adjutant and Dutch Captain placed under arrest.
April 19, no meat a little molasses, to a few grains of
rice.   April 27, a man shot in the leg for infringing
on the boundary.   May 2, our friend Shaw, the cav-
alryman, shot dead.   May 15, the singular cripple,
Chickamauga, shot dead in the stockade."

This witness further testified, that at one time the
men in the stockade could only get out to get wood
by paying the guard $3 in Federal money. May 18,
a general order signed by Wirz, was read to each
squad by the rebel sergeants, that if any of the men
tried to escape, the guns would be fired into the
stockade indiscriminately.   In the last of May the
prisoners had to lie on the bare ground, and they
were in a deplorable condition.   The dead were
laid outside of the tents where the sick and dying
could see them.   This witness only knew of one man
(Kelly, a seaman, who belonged to his squad,) who
ever came out of the hospital alive, after he went in
there.   Kelly was afterwards again taken to the hospital, and there died.   No rations were issued on the
3d of July, and on the 4th the rations were so full of
maggots that the prisoners threw them away.   On
the 13th day of July a man of the 20th Indiana was
shot dead by the guard at the dead-line.   On the 6th
of August, saw a man shot while he was reaching for
water over the dead line with his pan.   On the arri-
val of this witness at Andersonville, Wirz kept them

standing in the extreme heat of the sun for three hours
until he could count them.

Captain Wilson French, being sworn, testified that
he was a captain in the 17th Connecticut volunteers,
and was in Andersonville. The rations were not enough to sustain life. After the meal was sifted not
more than half a pint was left, and a half-pint of peas
after the dirt was taken out. Had they not been allowed by the sergeant who called the roll to buy vegetables, they would have starved. Bought sweet potatoes at fifteen dollars per bushel, and turnips at
twenty dollars per bushel. Bought meat, eggs and
biscuit. There seemed to be an abundance of those
things come to Andersonville. Had the officers not
been allowed to buy such things they would have
starved. The building they were confined in was
about sixty feet long and twenty-five feet wide. The
sixty-five officers were confined there. A one dollar
greenback was worth from thirteen to twenty dollars
in rebel money.

Robert Tart, being sworn, testified that he had
been in the 53d Pennsylvania regiment, and was a
prisoner at Andersonville. Had seen Wirz commit
acts of cruelty. About the first of May saw him
kick a man who was not able to stand up in line.
He kicked the man, and in a few days afterward the
man died. Heard Wirz order that men be put in the
chain-gang. One day Wirz's wife and daughters

were there, when he gave an order to have the men
in the chain-gang walk. His wife and daughters
laughed at it. Knew a man who was in the chain-
gang; he died shortly after being taken out. Wirz
fired his pistol at witness one day for being out of
line at roll-call; witness had a sore leg, and had sat
down; heard Wirz coming, and started to run; so as
to reach the line. Wirz said "hold on," and fired a
pistol at witness; witness got in line; Wirz came up
and said, "where is that man?" and declared that
we should have no rations until the man was found.
This witness then stepped out and said, "Captain
Wirz, I have a sore leg and cannot stand." Wirz
said he wished every Yankee's leg would rot off.

Samuel Andrews, being sworn, testified that he
was a prisoner at Andersonville. Had seen men vaccinated who became insane, and suffered the most intense agony from their sores. Saw two or three hundred cases of vaccination, causing large sores and making amputation necessary. Death was almost sure
to follow. Had seen men fall down dead. Two men
fell dead at the sink. This witness was not entirely
recovered from the effects of his confinement there.
Was in the hospital for a wound received when he
was captured. He attended to the wound himself.

Charles H. Russell was recalled, and testified that
he had seen acts of cruelty committed by a man,
James Duncan, who used to come in with the wagons

bringing in the bread, and whom witness understood
to be a rebel quartermaster. He here pointed out
Duncan in the court-room, and said: One day Duncan came in with the bread; a piece broke off; a prisoner standing by stooped down to pick it up. Duncan got down from the wagon and kicked and beat
the prisoner terribly. He died in a few days afterwards. Another day saw Duncan again beating a
man when he came in to give out bread. The prisoner whom he was beating, was a poor, half-witted
fellow. The first occurrence was about the 10th of
June, 1864.

The Court ordered that Duncan remain in the
court-room for the present.

W. W. Crandell, being sworn, testified that he
knew the man Duncan. He was termed quartermaster, and had charge of the cook-house. He used to
come in with the rations. About the 1st of October,
1864, witness was in the chain-gang; saw Duncan put
a man named Armstrong in the stocks; he took everything from him, including a picture of a sister that
he had. The man begged for the picture when he
was taken out of the stocks. Duncan told him that
he might consider himself lucky, if he got off with his
life.

Samuel N. Riker, being sworn, testified that he
was a prisoner at Andersonville. On arriving there,
was taken to Wirz's headquarters, and kept in the sun.

Many of them fell down, being unable to stand.—
Wirz ordered that all the prisoners be searched before
being put in the stockade. This witness was paroled
by Lieutenant Davis, and put on duty outside the
stockade. This witness knew of one case where Wirz
had picked out some pork; it spoiled. Wirz sent it
to the commissary and received good meat for it.—
The spoiled meat was issued to the prisoners. Knew
Duncan; he had charge of issuing and delivering the
rations to the prisoners. He was also a government
detective under the control of Captain Wirz. This
witness knew of Duncan being bribed to let men go.
He used to take meat from the soldiers' rations, and
carry it to his own house.

William B. Francis, being sworn, testified, that he
had been a prisoner at Andersonville; when witness
was first taken to Andersonville, they were kept
standing in the sun in front of Wirz's headquarters
about two hours. Orders came to take everything
from the prisoners; they were then searched and everything taken from them. This witness had ninety
six dollars, one dollar in gold, four photographs, and
two ambrotypes taken from him. Saw Wirz kick a
prisoner who was not able to stand up; he then ordered some of the other prisoners to take him away.
Wirz said to a prisoner that he would put him back
in the stockade where they were dying at the rate of
two hundred a day ; heard Wirz say that he gave the
men thirty days furlough for every Yankee they shot.

John A. Kane, being sworn, testified that he had
been in a California cavalry regiment. It was rain-
ing very hard at the time they arrived at Andersonville, 2 o'clock in the morning, and they were drawn
up in line four deep, and marched through water
knee-deep for half a mile, and then turned into the
stockade. This witness became so sick that he could
not attend roll-call, so his rations were stopped for
one day. He made up his mind, finally, to die, and
concluded he would not trouble his comrades to help
him to answer roll-call again, as they had previously
been doing. He was sent into hospital, where he saw
men brought in who were badly wounded. He here
referred to his memorandum book, and testified that
on May 2, 1864, a German, who belonged to a Pennsylvania regiment, was shot. The witness was in-
formed that the man was insane. An insane man
was shot and brought into the hospital. He when
alive would eat food which had not been digested.—
On July 25th, a rebel hospital guard shot a sick Union prisoner through the thigh, without warning, for
coming near his fire. He died from the effects afterwards. John Burk, 69th (Corcoran's) New York
cavalry, was shot in the right cheek, his tongue and
upper teeth being carried away, and three of his fingers nearly severed. The man took gangrene on the
root of his tongue, was taken in the surgeon's hospital and died. He said he was laying in his tent
when the guard fired at another man and hit him; he
died. This witness stated that he himself was a

cripple now from the effects of his imprisonment at
Andersonville.

Sergeant George W. Gray, being sworn, testified
that he belonged to the 7th Indiana Cavalry, and
was at Andersonville; when they arrived, they were
drawn up in line, and were told to take off their hav-
ersacks, knapsacks, canteens, etc., and pile them up in
front of the ranks; an officer then rode up and told
the guard to take what they wanted, and the prisoners could take what was left. The guard took all.
Did not know at that time that the officer on horse-
back was Captain Wirz. About the last of June or
the first of July, a prisoner who was wounded, named Underwood, of Company L, 7th Indiana cavalry,
went to the sutler and asked him for some medicine.
Wirz, who was standing by, said, "No, you can't have
it, except you pay me a dollar." Underwood pulled
out all the money he had, a $10 note, and gave it to
the Captain; after waiting for some time, he asked
for his change, when the Captain kicked him out of
the door. The man died afterwards. This witness
tried to escape about the last of August, but he was
hunted with the dogs, found and taken back. He
was then put into the stocks with his face turned upwards for four days in the sun. A young man named Stewart, of the 9th Minnesota cavalry, and witness went out with a dead body, and when they laid
it down, the Captain came up and asked by what authority they were there. Stewart replied, " By proper

authority." Wirz immediately shot him dead with
his revolver. The guard took $20 or $30 dollars
from his person, and the Captain then took it and carried it away with him. An order was received to parole the sick prisoners, and some of them were being
taken to the cars. This witness asked the Captain
to allow him to help some of the prisoners who could
not walk, but the request was not granted. An order
was given that any who fell between the stockade
and the cars should be bayoneted. This witness said
he saw many a poor soldier bayoneted as he was trying to crawl to the cars. He saw a man who had his
cheek torn off, and his arms and legs badly gnawed
by the dogs. He died within twenty-four hours.
This was in October, 1864.

The prisoner, Wirz, here raised himself on his hands
and knees on the sofa, and, addressing the witness,
said, " You did not see me there !"

The Judge Advocate here asked the accused to
rise to his feet, so that the witness could see him.—
This the prisoner, with much apparent agony succeeded in doing, when he again addressed the witness,
saying, " You never saw me there ; look good ; make
sure." The witness, hesitatingly, said he believed he
was the man. The prisoner here became perfectly
frantic, and appeared to be in agony from head to
foot, when the counsel and the guard induced him to
be seated, the counsel, Mr. Slade, telling him it would
be all right. The accused (drawing quick and heavy breaths) replied hysterically : "I know it will,

but, O God!" He was here handed his bottle of
stimulants, and given a drink of water, and the prison doctor, Mr. Ford, sent for. The accused was taken into an adjoining room.

Martin E. Aogin, being sworn, testified that he
had been a prisoner at Andersonville; the men were
were in a miserable condition, as bad as could be.
The men were so thick that they could scarcely elbow
their way. Some lay in their own filth, calling for
water and crying for food, but no attention was paid
them. He also testified to the quality of the food,
and its infamous effects, such as half-baked corn-
bread, which was sour, and the beef, when furnished,
was of an inferior quality. Men afflicted with the
scurvy would crawl upon the ground; the sight was
horrible. Very many were insufficiently clad and
had no shelter allowed on the ground. As to hounds,
he was brought back to prison by their agency. He
had seen Wirz, with hounds, trying to strike the
trail of a prisoner who had escaped from the prison
about the 8th of October, 1864. After the most ob-
scene abuse from Wirz, he was fastened by the neck
and feet, and remained there sixty-eight hours. He
heard Wirz give orders that he should not have food,
but he did get some from comrades who stole it. He
had known three comrades to be put in the stocks at
the same time. One man was put in the stocks because he asserted his manhood by resenting the abuse
of a Confederate soldier. When the prisoners were

14

being removed from Andersonville to Millen, this
witness saw Wirz take a man by the collar, because
he could not walk fast, (the man was so much worn
by disease he could not,) and throw him on his back
and stamp on him with his feet. He saw the man
bleeding, and he died a short time after in the dis-
secting room. He saw students in the pursuit of
knowledge, sawing upon the skulls of deceased prisoners, and opening the bodies.

J. D. Keiser, being sworn, testified that he was in
Andersonville; he arrived there with the first party
of four hundred, when there was sufficient accommo-
dation there; but as others were added, matters became bad, and the men began to be afflicted with the
diarrhoea, dysentery, scurvy and gangrene. They
lay on the ground and were not protected from the
weather. In April or May, 1864, supplies were received from the North. Some mouldy bread or cake
was thrown over the dead-line; while one man was
reaching beyond the line for this mouldy bread or
cake, a guard shot the man through the head. Saw
another man shot, after he was shot, in the abdomen.
He had seen men in the chain-gang with iron collars
round their necks; some of them were punished for
attempting their escape. Wirz was profane and
overbearing towards our men on the slightest provo-
cation; had seen men bucked by his order. This
witness had seen Gen. Winder at the prison, and one
of the prisoners rushed up to see him, when he told

our men to stand back, and gave orders to the guard
to fire on those who approached the gate nearer than
fifteen feet.

John Pasque, being duly sworn, testified that he
had been in the naval service of the United States,
and had been a prisoner at Andersonville; had seen
the chain-gang; four men were chained to a 68-lb.
solid shot; one man died there. Had heard the rebel guard say that every man who shot a Union prisoner inside the stockade got three month's extra pay
and thirty day's furlough.

W. W. Crandall, being sworn, testified that he belonged to the 4th Iowa Infantry; arrived at the Andersonville prison on the 28th of March, 1864; saw
two or three packs of hounds there; they were not
the common hounds; one or two bull or catch-dogs
were in each pack. This witness saw a man in his
detachment badly bitten in the calves of his legs by
the dogs; the man had tried to escape; he was
brought in and a ball attached to each foot: witness asked a surgeon to take the balls off, as the
prisoner's legs were much swollen. The balls were
kept to his feet about three weeks, when one was taken off. About the middle of August a man was
brought to the grave-yard which witness and others
believed was the one who had been in the stocks, al-
though he was quite black in the face. At the time
General Sherman was on the march near Atlanta,

Geo., the news came to the railroad depot at Andersonville, that Gen. Sherman, his whole staff, and
15,000 men had been captured, and that they were
on their way to Andersonville. Wirz said he could
take care of more Yankees there than any four regiments at the front : he had a good place to keep
them in.   One man was put in the spread-eagle stocks
for wanting to see his brother. In February or January, 1865, Wirz told witness that he would send a
lot of pork to the ware-house, which he wished ex-
changed for the best beef witness could pick out,
which he wanted sent to him.   It was stinking pork,
and the beef was good and intended for the prisoners.
When witness went into the stockade, he saw nothing
but living skeletons, and he remarked to his comrade
that those black men were in a miserable condition.
They were white men, he soon learned, smoked black.
They were so weak that they could not get to the
sink. Witness helped one of them there and back
again. Saw pies brought into the camp to those who
had money to pay for them. Saw one man eat a pie,
but his stomach would not hold it, and he vomited it
up. Another prisoner then grabbed it up and ate it.
The rebels used to rob the dead in the dead house, of
their clothing. They were laid in wagons as cord-
wood, when brought to the graves. From 15 to 25
were hauled at a load. Rebel officers who came to
to look at the graves, said the Yankees would make
good manure. They would plant a vineyard there,
and would invite their northern friends down to eat

the grapes with them, raised from the Yankee bones.
The spread-eagle stocks would hold two persons, the
others seven.

Louis Van Burch, being sworn, testified that he belonged to the 2d New York cavalry; saw sanitary
goods on the rebel officers; knew the pants by the
color and the blankets by the marks. Wirz told witness, when he arrived at Andersonville, to count off
his men. He did so, when he found he had two too
many, which fact he reported to Capt. Wirz, who said
with an oath that they were flankers. He put his pistol to witness's head and threatened to shoot him if
he allowed any more flankers to get in his squad. He
said with another oath that he could take care of more
Yankees there than Lee could at the front. One of
the men stepped out of the ranks to get a stick of
wood, when Wirz ordered the guard with an impre-
cation, to shoot him. The man, however, was in the
ranks again before the guard could shoot. Three men
were shot at the brook, in the latter part of August,
by one of the sentries, at one shot, while they were
getting water. One of the number was killed. Saw
another shot near the north side of the stockade. The
night before he had attempted to go to the dead-line
to be shot and thus have and end put to his misery;
witness tied him to his tent; in the morning he begged to be let loose, and promised he would not go to
the dead-line; he was released, and witness soon after
heard the report of a gun, when he went to look what

15

it meant. He saw that his man had gone to the dead-line, and was shot; this was in September, 1864; another was shot in the breast, as he was walking near the north gate of the stockade; witness understood from more than twenty men that Wirz shot him. He had passed over the dead-line to ask Wirz a question.

Dr. B. H. Vanderkift, being sworn, said that he was on duty at Annapolis from May 26, 1863, to May 28, 1865. He attended to more than 2000 of the returned prisoners at Andersonville. They were suffering from chronic diarrhoea, scurvy, and other diseases. Some were in a dying condition, and others had to be carried to the hospital before they acquired strength to be taken home. The disease from which death ensued more than from any other cause, was chronic diarrhoea, which resulted from insufficient and improper food and exposure. Very little attention was paid to their condition at Andersonville. He was shown photographs of a living skeleton, and said he had seen many of the prisoners returning in a similar condition.

CONFEDERATE TESTIMONY.

Col. Gibbs, sworn—Was the rebel commander of the post at Andersonville; Wirz had exclusive control of the prison, and he knew that there was food enough for all.

Hugh B. Harold, sworn—This witness had been in the rebel service as agent for the commissary, and furnished supplies to Andersonville. He testified that he had orders to retain all the provisions for Andersonville, and had plenty of transportation; had as much provision as he could ship, and there was no necessity of suffering at Andersonville on account of food.

James Van Valkensburg, sworn—Resided near Macon, Georgia. The crops raised in the South since the rebellion had been good. No cotton was planted. The ground was all used for provisions.

Col. D. S. Chandler, sworn—Testified that he had been in the service of the Confederate government, and had devoted about a week to the inspection of Andersonville. He had made calculations, and found that the prisoners in the stockade had about six square feet to each man—not a place six feet square, but one foot wide and six feet long. Green corn was plentiful, and could have been furnished. The drippings from the bake-house went to the brook which ran through the stockade.

Dr. J. J. Roy, sworn—Testified that he was on duly at Andersonville. The hospital was in a deplorable state, there not being a sufficient supply of tents and bunks. There were no comforts. He was told that there were between thirty and thirty-five thousand prisoners there. He did not find much difficulty in obtaining medicines, except a few of the rarer articles. The men presented the most horrible specimen of humanity ever seen. A few were affected with the worst forms of scurvy ; he attributed the sickness to long confinement, exposure, and the absence of the comforts of life. There were maggots in the swamp near the hospital, the malaria from which had a most fatal effect upon the patients. The insects, or white ants with wings, were such as result from decayed animal and vegetable matter. They were so numerous that it was dangerous for a man to open his mouth at sun-down.

Dr. B. J. Head was sworn, and testified that he was a physician, and was on duty at Andersonville. A Methodist minister named Davies, went up to see General Winder, and told him what the ladies of America were about to do. Mr. Davies said Winder said he would allow the ladies to send provisions.— The first and second lots were distributed. When the third lot was sent up, several ladies and witness went up to the prison with the goods. Lieutenant Reed ripped out a very profane word, and asked where those provisions were going. The reply was made that they were going to the Yankee hospital. Reed ripped out an oath and said they should not go. Several rebel officers were there. One said witness ought to be hung. Another said he ought to be shot. Witness told him it was a mission of mercy and charity ; he said he wished every Yankee sympathiser and every Yankee was in hell, and wound up by saying the provisions should not go to the hospital.— About this time, Lieut. Reed came running in, and said : " General, give me an order to have those goods confiscated !" Witness went to the ladies and told them it was best to go away, or Winder would arrest them all.

William N. Peeble, was sworn, and testified that he was detailed at Andersonville, under Col. Farnum,

in July, 1864, as a clerk.   He remained at Andersonville about three months.   Had seen Federal prisoners in the stocks.   One day, during a very heavy
rain, he rode up to a man who was in the stocks, and
held his umbrella over him, as he was nearly drown-
ed.   He afterwards went to Captain Wirz and asked
that the man be removed from the stocks, as he was
drowning.   Wirz said: "Let the Yankee drown, I
don't care."   Soon after some one went down and released the man.   The man appeared as though he was
drowning.   Witness resided about forty miles from
Andersonville.   The grain crop was very good in
1863.   Every planter received enough vegetables to
supply himself—some more.   There was a good crop
in 1864, a surplus.   In the northern part of the
State, in 1863, the crops were very good; had good
crops in 1864.   There was a railroad in the northern
part of the State.   Witness heard the rebel militia
in camp say the guard received furloughs for shooting Union prisoners.

Dr. Castline, being sworn, testified that he had
been in the Confederate army for the past two years;
was on duty at Andersonville as a surgeon of the 3d
Georgia Reserves; occasionally saw the prisoners in
the stockade; their condition was deplorable; the
stench was horrible; had seen negroes at work about
there; had seen vegetables in market there—cab-
bage, potatoes, cucumbers, melons, etc. ; had seen
vegetables in camp; had no trouble in getting medicine; on one occasion saw Capt. Wirz strike a man
once or twice ; saw the dogs bite a man on one occasion. the man was up in a tree, and he was ordered
down.   The man came down and was bitten by the
dogs.   The prisoner was there at the time.

Ambrose Spencer, being sworn, testified that he
resided near Americus, Ga., about nine miles from Andersonville; had resided there for the past five years,
16

and frequently visited Andersonville, during the year 1864 there was uncommon supply of vegetables.— Every day the trains were loaded with persons carrying vegetables to Andersonville. Some officer at Andersonville had agents at Americus to purchase vegetables.

The range of the thermometer during the summer of 1864 was very high. Witness thought it had been as high as 110 in the shade. On one occasion witness put the thermometer in the sun in the month of June, 1864. It ranged 127 and 130. The winter of 1864 and 1865 was the coldest winter they had in Georgia for twenty-five years. Witness had seen the thermometer about 25 degrees. Witness was aroused one night, it was very cold, he opened the window and found an escaped prisoner from Andersonville.— Witness went down and brought him in : he was nearly frozen and poorly clad. Witness looked at the thermometer, it was 18 degrees above zero.

At one time a general effort was made by the ladies of the country to relieve the prisoners. A large amount of provisions were collected and sent up to Andersonville. Witness thought the effort failed.— General Winder refused to allow the provisions to be carried in. Spencer had a conversation with the General. He said he believed the whole country was becoming Yankee, and the effort to relieve the prisoners was a slur on the Confederate Government, and he would put a stop to it. The witness told him he did not think it showed Yankee or Union feeling to have feelings of humanity ; he said it was best for the Yankee to die there. He used such language toward the ladies that no gentleman could listen to it in the presence of his wife without resenting it : it was such language as was not fit to be repeated here in the presence of ladies.

Winder indicated that he could make the women

loyal to the Confederate Government by putting them in a certain condition. The witness heard the prisoner remark that if he had his way a house should be built there, and the ladies put into it for a certain infamous purpose, which witness did not like to repeat. The witness knew Turner, the keeper of the hounds. Turner told witness that he was making money, more than he could by cultivating his ground. Wirz was his paymaster.

The witness asked Winder if he was going to erect barracks or shelter. The witness then asked him why he cut down the trees. He replied: "I am going to build a pen here that will kill more Yankees than they do at the front."

Dr. John C. Bates, who was contract surgeon under the rebel government at Andersonville from September 22d, '64, to March 26th, '65, being sworn, testified as follows:

On going into ward fifteen of the hospital, I saw a number of men, and was rather shocked. Many of them were lying partially naked, dirty and lousy, in the sand. Others were crowded together in small tents, the latter unserviceable at the best. I examined all who were placed in my charge. I enquired into the rations and talked about them. The sufferers frequently asked me for a tablesoonful of salt, or orders for a little siftings that came out of meal, as they wanted to make some bread.

The men would gather around me and ask for a bone. The living were supplied with the clothing of those who died.

At the time I went, there were 2,000 or 2,200 sick. I judge 20,000 or 25,000 prisoners were crowded together. Some had made holes and burrowed in the earth. Those under the sheds were doing comparatively well; I saw but little shelter except what ingenuity had devised. I found them suffering with scurvy, dropsy, diarrhea, gangrene, pneumonia, and other diseases. Prisoners, when dead, were laid in wagons, head foremost, to be carried off; I don't know how they were buried. The effluvia from the hospital was very offensive. If by accident my hand was abraded, I would not go into the hospital without putting a blister over the affected part. If persons whose systems were reduced by inanition should perchance stump a toe or scratch a hand, the next report to me was gangrene, so potent was the regular hospital gangrene. The prisoners were thickly confined in the stockade like ants and bees. The dogs referred to, were to hunt the prisoners who escaped. Fifty per cent. of those who died might have been saved. I feel safe in saying seventy-five might have been saved, had the patients been properly cared for. I found persons lying dead sometimes among the living. Thinking they merely slept, I went to wake them up, but found they had taken their everlasting sleep. This was in the hospital. I judge it was about the same in the stockade.

The foregoing is the testimony of men who were in the service of the rebel government.

MISCELLANEOUS TESTIMONY.

Testimony of a Georgian---Brutality Unparalleled.

A Georgia planter, who lived near Andersonville, and had means of accurate knowledge as to the treatment of our prisoners, gives to the New York Evening Post the following:

The prison at Andersonville is a stockade about eighteen feet high, the posts comprising it being sunk in the ground five feet; it originally comprised an area of eighteen acres, but was subsequently enlarged to twenty-seven acres. The inclosure is upon the side of a hill, looking toward the south, at the foot of which is a small brook about five feet wide, and as many inches deep, which furnished the water for the use of the prisoners. Within this enclosure were turned the prisoners as they arrived, and left to provide for themselves, there being no shelters, or arbors, or any kind of protection afforded by tree or otherwise against the burning rays of the Southern sun, the furious storms, or the freezing winters.

The position was selected by Capt. Winder, a son of Gen. John H. Winder, who was sent from Richmond for that purpose in the latter part of 1863. When it was suggested to him by a disinterested but humane spectator of his operations, that it would perhaps be better to leave the trees standing within the proposed stockade, as they would afford shade to the prisoners, he replied: "That was just what he was going to do : he was going to make a pen for the——Yankees, where they could rot faster than they could be sent there."

And admirably did he accomplish his mission.

The first commandant of the post was Colonel Parsons, who was soon succeeded by John H. Winder, with his son as Adjutant, his nephew as Commissary and sutler, and Captain Henry Wirz in immediate command of the prisoners. There were generally stationed there for guard duty from three to six regiments of infantry, with one company of artillery, having a battery of six pieces, according to the exigencies of the case, the number of prisoners there confined, or the fears entertained of an attempt to set them at liberty by raiding parties of United States troops.

17

When prisoners were first received it was usual to subject them to a search for money, valuables, etc., which were ostensibly to be restored when they were released from captivity, but which in reality went into the pockets of those who controlled the prison. Notwithstanding a law of the Confederacy, expressly prohibiting the dealing in "greenbacks," yet the initiated, a few whose 'loyalty' was unquestioned, could always obtain for a consideration all the greenbacks that they required.

The writer of this was the foreman of the last grand jury which was impanneled for Sumner County, Ga., and in the performance of his duties he had to investigate a large number of presentments for dealing in the forbidden currency, which were brought against poor Union men in every instance. Struck by this fact, he resolved to examine, as his position gave him a right to do, into all the circumstances: where the money originally came from, who did the selling of it, indeed the whole modus operandi; and he elicited the fact above stated; how the money was obtained; that the Winders and Wirz were the principals, acting through the subordinates in gathering bushels of plums, in the way of premiums, etc. Meanwhile the prisoners were left to the tender mercies of their jailors and commissary for their food, which might have been improved in quantity at least, if their money had been left in their own possession.

At first it was customary to send a wagon into the stockade every morning at 10 o'clock, loaded with the rations of the day —bacon and corn bread, nothing else; but as the number of the prisoners increased and the greed of gain grew upon the trio just mentioned, the corn bread was reduced in its quality, being then manufactured of equal proportions of ground field peas and corn, unbolted, unsifted, uncleansed, indeed, from the dirt and trash which peas naturally accumulate; and at last when the number of prisoners increased to 37,000, the meat rations per week were reduced to a piece of bacon for each man, about three inches long and two wide, with one pone of the bread above described, per day. Then, also, the custom of carrying the prisoners' food in the stockade in wagons was abolished. They drove up to the gates, which were slightly opened, and the scanty food, foul and unhealty as it was, was thrown inside by the guard, to be scrambled for by the wretched prisoners, the strongest and those nearest the gate getting the largest share, the weak and sickly getting none.

I have mentioned the brook which ran through the lower part of the stockade, and which supplied the water for drinking and washing. This brook has its rise in a swamp not far from the prison, and at no time, certainly not for a lengthened period, was the water suitable or healthy, but when the fæces and filth, the drainage of the whole camp of prisoners, came to be superadded to the natural unfitness of the water for drinking or cleansing purposes, my readers can judge what thirst was assuaged, or fever cooled, or throbbing temples washed, by this floating stream of disease and filth! At any time, under the most rigid hygienic restrictions, it is difficult to maintain health and cleanliness among a large number of men—what do you think was the condition of 37,000 half-naked, half-starved men, without any police regulations, under no moral or restraining influences? If the remnant, who were finally allowed to pass out of this military Golgotha, were not wild beasts, unwashed, be-fouled devils, no thanks are to be given to Captain Wirz for lack of effort to produce such a consummation.

When it rained, as it does in that climate almost continually during the spring and fall months, the soil within the inclosure was one mass of loblolly, soft mud, at least fifteen inches in depth, through which stalked and stalked and staggered the gaunt, half-clad wretches thus confined. The stench from the prison could be perceived for two miles, and farmers living in the neighborhood began to fear for the health of their families. As a consequence of this, the hospitals—facetious was Wirz in his horrible humanity—were crowded to repletion with the emaciated, starved and diseased men who were trundled into them.

The hospitals were constructed of logs, unhewn, the interstices unfilled and open, admitting the rain, without floors, cots, bunks, or blankets, filthy and fetid with the festering, putrid bodies of the sick, the dying and the dead. Words fail, language is impotent to describe one of these dens of disease and death. I once mustered the courage, impelled by the earnest entreaties of Northern friends, to visit one who was tenderly reared, and walked in the best ranks of Connecticut society.— I believed I had seen before this what I deemed to be human wretchedness in its worst forms. I thought that I could nerve myself to witness mortal agony and wretchedness and destitution, as I had heard it described. But if the condemned horrors of a hundred "black holes" had been brought before my mind to prepare me for the ordeal, they would have failed to realize the facts as I saw them face to face.

Convicted by the horrible fact that was a stench in his nostrils, Gen. Winder, then Commissary General of Prisons, but having his headquarters at Andersonville, was forced by decency, not humanity, for this he himself asserted, to ask the aid of the Presiding Elder of the Methodist Church of that circuit, to adopt some means to alleviate the miseries and sooth the wretchedness of the poor inmates of that Andersonville hospital. This gentleman invoked the co-operation of the women of Sumner county, who responded with clothing and necessaries only, for these alone were allowed to the amount of four wagon loads. Upon the day appointed, four ladies, with their husbands, went to the Prison and sought from the Provost Marshall a pass, to take the benefactions to the sick prisoners. It was refused with a curse! The party proceeded to Winder's headquarters, where Henry Wirz was in company with the General. The demand for a pass was repeated. Understand, the ladies were present, and the reasons given why the party were there in accordance with Winder's special request. To their astonishment, they were met with this reply: "G—d d—n you, have you turned Yankees here?"

"No, General," responded the spokesman of the party, "I am not, as you know, nor are any here present; we have come, as you requested us, through Rev. Dr. D., to bring necessary articles for the Federal hospital, and ask for a pass for the purpose of delivering them."

"It's a d—d lie! I never gave permission for anything of the kind! Be off with you, all of you."

As if this fearless display of martial valor and gentlemanly bearing was not sufficient, Henry Wirz essayed to and did eclipse his general in profanity and indecency; and I here assert that if the lowest sinks of the most abandoned parts of our city were gleaned they could not surpass the ribald vulgarity and finished profanity of this jailor, exhibited in the presence of refined and loyal ladies. Shocked, terrified, beaten to the very dust with mortification, the party retired, and foiled in their efforts to succor the sick or alleviate the tortures of the dying Union soldier, they gave their load of clothing and food to a passing column of Federal prisoners on their way to another place, Millen. They at least had the satisfaction of knowing that some were benefited, even if they had failed in their efforts for those who most needed their assistance.

During last winter, which was unusually cold for Georgia, when the ice made an inch thick, no shelter, no blankets or clothes, no wood were provided for the wretched inmates of that prison. Squads—to the number of thirty—were permitted to go out under guard daily, for one hour, without axes or any cutting tools, to gather the refuse and rotten wood in the forests; and if they outstaid their time, they were tried by drum head court-martial, charged with violating their parole, and if found guilty, were hung! I myself saw three bodies hanging who were thus executed.

Testimony of a Female—Shocking Details!

'The Chattanooga "Gazette" has the following statement from a Mrs. E. M. Warren, a nurse in the rebel hospitals of Georgia:

Mrs. Warren was sent from the Empire Hospital, at Atlanta, on or about the 1st of December, to lend her aid to the sick and wounded at Albany Hospital, Doherty county, Ga. On her way thither she visited Andersonville, at which place she stopped over for several days, for the ostensible purpose of waiting on the sick, wounded, and prisoners; and to learn from personal observation, whether the sick, &c., were being treated in such a cruel and inhuman manner as reported and whispered among the more Christian and human people of Atlanta. Mrs. W. visited the sick, wounded and prisoners, but ere she had half completed her contemplated tour, her heart so sickened at what she saw in that foul den, that she covered her eyes with horror, and turned away and sought refuge beyond the limits of the place where naught could be seen but man's inhumanity to man.

She saw half clad living skeletons, devoid of shoes and stockings, standing upon the frosty ground, and would occasionally lift their feet goose-like, and wrap them in the tattered rags that hung about their person, and press their feet close to the body for its warmth to shield them from the frost. Men could be seen engaged in carrying the dead bodies from the straw pallets of the den—stacking them up at the entrance to be carried out for interment, without coffins, friends, or comrades to follow the corpse to its resting place.

Inhuman wretches were there, clad in gray, with muskets overlooking these sad and solemn movements of the dead, and should one of the prisoners engaged in moving the dead, fall under the weight imposed upon him, the wretches in gray would stick them with their bayonets and curse them for neglect of duty; and not unfrequently the bodies of soldiers were carried away for interment before life was extinct.

She further stated, however, that while in company with several ladies, she saw Wirz, at which time she addressed him and remonstrated against such inhuman treatment of the prisoners under his command. The colloquy terminated by Mrs. W. calling Wirz a "Dutch Monster." Wirz replied by saying that "several ladies of Andersonville had recently very mysteriously left the town for making similar expressions, and you

18

may go in the same way if you persist in making such expressions."

Mrs. Warren became frightened at the remark of Wirz, and
the accompanying ladies advised her to leave Andersonville at
once, for if she remained Wirz would certainly do as he said
or intimated—put her out of the way.

Mrs. W. left town the following morning and went direct to Albany, Doherty county, Georgia, where she entered the hospital as matron.

On or about the 15th of December, the prisoners of Andersonville were moved to Albany, in consequence of an expected
advance of the Federal cavalry. At Albany, the prisoners, or
many of them, were forced to climb the China trees at that
place, and eat the dry berries, which are very astringent, and
said to be poisonous. The China tree berries of the South are
never eaten by any one under any circumstances.

At this place the prisoners were camped in an open field,
grown up with sedge grass, without tents or blankets, and with
scarcely sufficient clothing to cover their nakedness. On account of the severe cold the prisoners dug holes in the ground,
and buried themselves as best they could to shield themselves
from the inclement weather. The prisoners remained at this
place three weeks with barely sufficient food to sustain life, in
consequence of which many of them became so weak and faint
that they could not walk.

At the close of the time above stated, the prisoners were obliged to return to Andersonville. Those who could not march
did not fall in when so ordered, but remained in the camp in
their holes, covered with sedge grass, (which had been found
in the field, and was gathered by hand, and thrown upon the
loose rails over their holes in the ground, forming a covering
that shielded them from the frosts of winter,) to be buried alive
as Wirz ordered the camp to be fired, and many a poor, sick, faint
prisoner was burned to death on the spot, and many afterward
died in consequence of their injuries.

The following is written by a lady traveling in the East:

"I saw at New York a lady with her husband, who had
been two years in prison. I never shall forget the sight. He
was a mere living skeleton, and a maniac. She took care of
him as of a child. Sometimes he thought she was one of the
guard; then he would think she was the doctor, and he would
ask her to kill him; then he would ask for bread. But enough
of this."

No amplification can add to the horrors of that simple tale,
which is copied in the exact words of the writer.

CONCLUSION.

I will conclude this book by drawing from the inimitable pen of Clara Barton, the soldier's friend:

"After this, whenever any man who has lain a prisoner within the stockade of Andersonville, would tell you of his sufferings; how he fainted, scorched, drenched, hungered, sickened, was scoffed, scourged, hunted and persecuted, though the black tale be long and twice told; as you would have your own wrongs appreciated, your own woes pitied, your own cries for mercy heard, I charge you listen and believe him. However definitely he may have spoken, know that he has not told you all. However strongly he may have outlined, or deeply he may have colored his picture, know that the reality calls for a better light and a nearer view than your clouded, distant gaze will ever get.

"And your sympathies need not be confined to Andersonville, while similar horrors glared in the sunny light and spotted the flower-girt garden fields of that whole desperate, misguided and bewildered people. Wherever stretched the form of a Union

prisoner, there arose the signal for cruelty and the
cry of agony, and there, day by day, grew the skeleton graves of the nameless dead.

"Yet, braving and enduring all this, some thousands have returned to you ; but they bear with them
the seeds of disease and death sown in that fatal clime
and ripening for an early harvest.

"With occasional exceptions, they will prove to be
short-lived and enfeebled men, and whether they ask
it or not, will deserve at your hands no ordinary share
of kindly consideration.

"The survivor of a rebel prison has endured and
suffered what you never can, and what, I pray God,
your children never may.

"With less of strength and more of sad and bitter
memories, he is with you now, to earn the food no
longer denied him.

"If he ask 'leave to toil,' give it him before it is
too late.

"If he need kindness and encouragement, bestow
them freely, while you may.

"Finally, yet tremulously, let me hasten to com-
mend to the grateful consideration of this noble, gen-
erous people, alike, the soldier who has given his
strength, the prisoner who has sacrificed his health,
the widow who offered up her husband, the orphan
that knows only that his father went out to battle
and comes no more home forever, and the lonely, distant grave of the martyr who sleeps alone in a strange
soil, that freedom and peace might be ours."

We Never Can Forget It.

[SELECTED.]

[We regret that we are unable to give the name of the
author of this beautiful poem.]

Oh, we never can forget it,
   Thro' the many years to come,
How we lingered, starved and waited
   In the prison far from home!
How at night we longed for morning
   And the morning brought despair,
As we breathed the pois'nous vapors
   Of the vile and stagnant air.

How we suffered in our weakness—
   Freezing, starving--none can tell;
Stag'ring near the fatal "dead line,"
   Where so many gladly fell;
Gazing into ghastly faces,
   When all joy and hope had fled;
Longng, dying for the fire light,
   With no shelter, clothes, or bed.

Oh we never can forget it,
   No that prison-pen so bare,
Where we watched in weary silence
   For our scanty wretched fare:
For the loathsome, rancid bacon,
   And the bitter, mouldy bread,
That we clutched with bloodless fingers,
   Like the fingers of the dead.

How we wondered in our anguish
   If our kindred were no more—
If the starry banner floated
   Now as proudly as before—
If our mothers, sisters, brothers,
   Prayed for us when they did kneel?
Thus when thinking of our home-scenes
   How the giddy brain would reel!

Oh we never can forget it,
   When the gates were opened wide,
When we saw the Union Banner,
   And our friends were at our side;
How we laughed and cried like children,
   Though we tried to feel like men,
As we shouted in our gladness
   "Home, yes, home; sweet home again."

Buried at Andersonville.

COPIED FROM THE OFFICIAL RECORDS AT WASHINGTON.

NOTE.—The ° denotes a Corporal; ° ° a Sergeant. The figures on the left indicate the number of the grave.

NEW YORK—continued.

519 Rafferty, M, 182, Co G, died Apr 12.
2584 Rafferty, P, 5 cav, Co M, died June 26.
11380 Rafferty, T, 5 artill, Co B, died Oct 28.
4508 Raker, L, 1 cav, Co M, died Aug 8.
8751 Ranch, J, 100, Co D, died July 21.
10675 Randall, John, 99, Co A, died Oct 12.
6508 Ralinger, J, 47, Co D, died Aug 22.
6794 Rangheart, John, 100, Co A, died Aug 28.
7778 Rastifer, John, 100, Co A, died Sept 4.
4916 Rattery, John, 104, Co I, died July 29.
10657 Ray, C, 2 cav, Co B, died Oct 14.
10946 Ray, E S, 154, Co A, died Oct 3.
4856 Raymard, P, 135, Co F, died July 30.
2425 Rattersboom, J, 8 artill, Co K, died July 17.
8650 Ramsey, Isaac, 66, Co I, died July 4.
1905 Ramsay, Hiram, 81, Co K, died May 21.
2186 Reamer, W C, 111, Co B, died June 19.
2680 Redman, J, 8 artill, Co K, died July 3.
11095 R do, D V, 5 cav, Co M, died Oct 31.
7212 Reed, F A, 64, Co E, died Aug 30.
8574 Reed, J, 140, Co H, died Sept 12.
400 Reed, S G, 13, Co D, died April 6.
6041 Reed, W D, 146, Co H, died Aug 16.
10583 Reed, W J, 41, Co I, died Oct 2.
8492 Reed, William, 14 artill, Co I, died Sept 11.
7809 Reets, John, 52, Co A, died Aug 31.
5694 Reeve, G, 152, Co G, died Aug 15.
1080 Reeves, John, 57, Co H, died June 6.
10467 Redmoul, J, 45, Co C, died Oct 7.
10911 Regler, W H, 22 cav, Co M, died Oct 14.
9128 Reiley, P C, 164, Co H, died Sept 16.
7195 Renback, C, 89, died Aug 29.
12455 Rebman, J, 89, Co C, died Jan 15, '65.
8421 Rencormann, J R, 5 cav, Co B, died Sept 11.
6630 Randall, A B, 76, Co F, died Sept 20.
3363 Rensen, C, 2 cav, Co M, died July 15.
5309 Reynolds, C, 155, Co M, died Sept 6.
6799 Reynolds, O S, 85, Co E, died Aug 25.
10565 Reynolds, Samuel, 92, Co H, died Oct 6.
6850 Reynolds, Wm, 140, Co I, died Aug 31.
6346 Reddy, J D, 65, Co I, died Aug 28.
4815 Rice, F, 39, Co I, died July 30.
8077 Rich, T D, 24 battery, died July 9.
12999 Rich, J, 89, Co C, died Dec 15.
8561 Richey, R, 66, Co C, died July 18.
8497 Rider, B, 176, Co E, died June 24.
6005 Rhonevault, R H, 21, Co B, died Sept 6.
11904 Rohm, W, 7 artill, Co C, died Nov. 7.
8991 Richistine, C°, 182, Co D, died July 24.
8817 Richards, A, 59, Co D, died Aug 11.
6574 Richards, A, 41, Co E, died Aug 14.
12443 Richards, A, 9, Co C, died Dec 7.
8893 Richards, H, 47, Co E, died July 31.
7676 Richards, N J†, 146, Co C, died Sept 2.
4340 Richardson, H M, 20 cav, Co M, died July 29.

9751 Ross, A, 1 cav, Co M, died Sept 25.
11963 Ross, J H, 191, Co G, died Nov 11.
5980 Rosenberger, John, 4, Co D, died Aug 17.
8616 Rosser, Lewis, 64, Co A, died July 20.
3934 Rosenburg, J, 95, Co A, died July 5.
8757 Rosson, Chas, 24 cav, Co E, died Sept 14.
12356 Roswell, J, 52, Co K, died Dec 10.
737 Ross, Jacob, 151, Co A, died April 26.
1940 Row, W J, 120, Co B, died June 14.
5097 Roth, Louis, 39, Co D, died Aug 9.
8604 Rothwell, M,° 20 cav, Co M, died Sept 12.
8792 Rouge, Wm, bugler, 12 cav, Co F, died July 21.
7709 Rowbotham, R, 11 cav, Co L, died Sept 3.
5857 Rowell, J E, 70, Co G, died Aug 16.
3493 Rowell, L N, 99, Co H, died July 17.
59 Roberts, A B,† 8 cav, Co B, died Mar 19.
2609 Ruddin, O, 120, Co H, died June 28.
867 Rudler, Wm, 120, Co M, died May 3.
40 Rue, Newton,† 8 cav, Co A, died Mar 13.
6667 Runey, F, 69, Co E, died Sept 12.
12635 Russ, John, 2, Co K, died Feb 10, '65.
6856 Russell, J,° 7 artill, Co A, died Sept 15.
8004 Ryan, D, 106, Co D, died Aug 8.
8599 Ryan, J, 95, Co E, died Sept 12.
8741 Ryan, J, 22 cav, Co M, died Sept 14.
7358 Ryan, Owen, 12, Co A, died Aug 30.
4763 Rynoch, John, 66, Co I, died Aug 5.
6413 Ryson, John, 7 artill, Co L, died Aug 22.
6905 Ryne, J M, 39, Co H, died Aug 9.
684 Rush, John, 111, Co E, died April 28.
7284 Sackett, R S, 85, Co G, died Aug 30.
1929 Sadley, M, 77, Co H, died June 14.
1880 Safford, B J, 34 battery, died June 19.
11870 Salsbury, H, 1 artill, Co M, died Nov. 6.
10652 Salisbury, E, 16, Co D, died Oct 11.
10028 Samlett, —, 18 cav, Co I, died Oct 14.
10650 Samet, W, 15, Co H, died Oct 18.
8769 Sampson, J, 108, Co K, died July 22.
846 Sanders, Charles,° 9 mil, Co A, died April 2.
8616 Sanders, J, 98, Co C, died July 23.
9857 Sanders, J, 12 cav, Co A, died Sept 27.
4433 Saudford, P O, 7 artill, Co L, died July 31.
2841 Sanghin, J, 12 cav, Co F, died June 22.
7740 Sawyer, J, 2 cav, Co L, died Sept 3.
11283 Sayles, A, 22 cav, Co E, died Oct 31.
3612 Scaman, A,° 85, Co H, died July 19.
10856 Seaman, A, 2 artill, died Oct 18.
1372 Sears, F, 2 cav, Co E, died May 26.
6120 Seagher, J, 6, Co M, died Aug 10.
4835 See, Henry, 11, Co K, died July 30.
8524 Seeley, A J, 140, Co A, died Sept 15.
11374 Seeley, C B, 15, Co H, died Oct 24.
4256 Seeley, Thomas, 100, Co F, died July 29.
10097 Segam, E, 5 cav, Co K, died Sept 29.
4904 Seigler, George, 10, died July 29.
7458 Seiglo, John R, 120, Co K, died Sept 1.
11896 Seisou, H, 39, Co C, died Nov 6.
8467 Serrier, R, 40, Co C, died July 17.
1746 Serine, C, 4 cav, Co M, died June 8.
629 Settle, Henry, 99, Co H, died April 1.
9828 Seyman, F, 1 cav, Co A, died Sept 27.
5051 Seard, Louis, 77, Co E, died Aug 17.
6868 Schayier, J W, 21 cav, Co M, died Aug 26.
10794 Schadt, Theodore, 100, Co A, died Oct 19.
5857 Scheck, B, 2 cav, Co G, died July 16.
8190 Schomerhorn, H, 120, Co G, died July 19.
11065 Schrapp, M, 7 artill, Co F, died Nov 11.

New York state suffered the most casualties at Andersonville Prison.

12196 Riuker, M, 2 artil, Co M, died Nov 29.
8153 Riukhor, J, 85, Co E, died Sept 8.
415 Rikel, Ro'vrt, 125, Co G, died April 7.
13389 Riley, I, 73, Co K, died Jan 2 '65.
2836 Riley, J, 99, Co C, died July 4.
5031 Riley, John, 176, Co O, died Aug 8.
6347 Riley, John, 39, Co D, died Aug 31.
11168 Ripley, F A, 153, Co C, died Oct 19.
11760 Ripp, W, 42, Co B died Nov 8.
8514 Rising, O, 76, Co B, died July 18.
10810 Risley, George W, 47, Co G, died Oct 4.
3555 Ritcher, F†, 183, Co D, died June 27.
7245 Ritson, S, 18 cav, Co E, died Aug 39.
9334 Ritsmillin, John, 115, died Sept 19.
1773 Roach, F, 99, Co F, died June 9.
1843 Roach, Charles, 85, Co B, died June 11.
3354 Robberger, PH, 46, Co B, died June 26.
11195 Roberson, U A, 133, Co B, died Oct 20.
2546 Robertson, W H, 134, Co B, died June 24.
6554 Robertson, W M, 96, Co B, died Sept 12.
9970 Robinson, H, 39, Co K, died Sept 28.
7607 Robinson, A, 111, Co I, died Sept 2.
8690 Robinson, H O, 95, Co I, died July 31.
6419 Robinson, John, 115, Co A, died Aug 22.
27 Robins, L,° 154, Co K, died Mar 8.
7063 Roberts, A, 173, Co O, died Sept 8.
7365 Rockwell, N C, 14 artil, Co D, died Sept 2.
8818 Rockfellar, R E, 85, Co D, died July 23.
11843 Rockfellar, H, 16 artil, Co M, died Oct 28.
3959 Rock, F, 6 artil Co F, died July 25.
4930 Rogers, A, 7 artil, Co I, died July 31.
6059 Rogers, A, 125, Co H, died Aug 18.
8791 Rogers, G, musician, 85, Co F, died Aug 15.
3011 Rogers, James, 132, Co H, died July 7.
4387 Rogers, H O, 85, Co O, died July 30.
6369 Rogers, H J, 2 artil, Co E, died Sept 10.
4912 Rogers, M, 43, Co D, died Aug 6.
7306 Rogers, O S,† 85, Co C, died Aug 29.
6634 Rogers, Thomas, 12, Co F, died Aug 26.
11773 Romer, F, 9, Co A, died Nov 3.
8408 Rook, G, 6 artil, Co E, died Sept 11.
9068 Rooney, John, 152, Co G, died Sept 26.
9103 Rooney, M, 132, Co F, died Sept 16.
8933 Rooney, P, 2 artil, Co O, died Sept 16.
5569 Root, A N, 85, Co O, died Aug 14.
2026 Root, W T, 120, Co H, died July 7.
1785 Root, Legrand, 24 battery, died June 6.
10278 Rose, A, 16, Co L, died Oct 2.
9550 Roseoranns, J E, 125, Co H, died Sept 28.
8171 Ross, O, 23 cav, Co A, died Sept 5.
3874 Ross, E, 3, 111, Co I, died July 24.
8591 Ross, David, 27, Co D, died Aug 14.
6741 Ross, G, 76, Co K, died Aug 24.

2795 Schermashle, B, 170, Co A, died July 2.
1935 Schlotesser, J, 91, Co H, died May 24
11515 Schlotesser, J,† 1, Co L, died Oct 26
9576 Schmaker, John, 39, Co B, died Sept 28.
10991 Schmaley, J, 1, Co G, died Oct 16.
10550 Schmeager, A, 39, Co A, died Oct 9.
8511 Schneider, Charles, 39, Co A, died Aug 11.
6505 Schockney, T T, 24 battery, died Sept 12.
8706 Schofield, J, 7, Co H, died Sept 15.
2441 Scholl, John, 54, Co D, died June 25.
11493 Schriber, H, 59, Co I, died Oct 24.
7814 Schroder, G, 7 artil, Co E, died Sept 4.
8530 Schrum, J, 15 artil, Co K, died Sept 13.
1070 Schrimer, Wm, 20, Co B, died May 18.
4380 Schware, F, 13 cav, Co K, died July 30.
6613 Schwick, A, 66, Co G, died Aug 28.
4659 Scott, J C,† 85, Co K, died Aug 6.
6657 Scott, P O, 14 cav, Co G, died Aug 26.
6692 Scott, W W, 2 cav, Co F, died Sept 13.
8390 Sibble, W, 146, Co G, died Sept 9.
4363 Sick, R, 5, Co E, died July 31.
4557 Sickler, E, 7 artil, Co E, died Aug 3.
3310 Sickles, A, 120, Co D, died July 19.
11950 Siddell, G, 40, Co H, died Nov 10.
12364 Simmons, A, 8, artil, Co H, died Dec 13.
6564 Simmons, C O,† 85, Co B, died Aug 21.
8316 Simon, H, 146, Co B, died Sept 10.
6284 Simons, H L,† 85 Co E, died Aug 20.
142 Simondinger, B, 155, Co I, died Mar 24.
249 Simpson, D, 99, Co H, died Mar 30.
6345 Sisson, P V,† 22 artil, Co M, died Aug 21.
10067 Shaat, J, 50, Co A, died Sept 30.
201 Shae, Pat, drummer, 61, Co M, died Mar 28.
4601 Shaffer, M, 7 artil, died Aug 5.
4584 Shaffer, J, 66, Co E, died Aug 2.
782 Shafer, H, 108, Co F, died Apr 28.
6747 Shaughnessey, J, 6 cav, Co A, died Aug 24.
4446 Shannan, E, 6 artil, Co H, died Aug 1.
8648 Shank, S W, 24 battery, died Aug 14.
290 Shaw, Alexander, 3 artil, Co K, died Apr 1.
9667 Shaw, T I, 15 cav, Co M, died Sept 24.
12814 Shaw, W, 7 artil, Co F, died Mar 25.
7660 Shay, John, 69, Co B, died Sept 3.
3860 Sheldon, M, 7 artil, Co B, died July 15.
4247 Shepardson, L,° 22 cav, Co E, died July 29.
5474 Shaw, J, 2 cav, Co E, died Aug 18.
7798 Shuler, Chas, 52, Co G, died Sept 4.
8335 Shaw, M, 76, Co D, died Sept 10.
9924 Sheppard, W H, 9, Co F, died Sept 28.

List of New York Union Soldiers buried at Andersonville, contd.

Smith, Wm, 99, Co M, died March 24.
335 Smith, Wm, 3 artll, Co K, died April 2.
539 Smith, Wm, 104, Co A, died April 14.
612 Smith, Wm, 106, Co B, died April 30.
7350 Smith, Wm. 3, Co L, died Sept 3.
10164 Smith, Wm, 76, Co K, died Oct 1.
12894 Smith, H, 7, Co C, died Jan 5, '65.
8706 Snedegar, A J, 111, Co D, died July 31.
7173 Sayder, A, 35, Co E, died Aug 30.
4446 Snyder, B, 2, Co B, died Aug 1.
10075 Snyder, Wm, 1 dragoons, Co E, died Sept 30.
1319 Sombeck, Geo, 52, Co I, died May 26.
5160 Somers, John, 3, Co B, died Aug 6.
3773 Sopher, James, 133, Co F, died July 2.
2408 Sopher, S, 102, Co K, died June 24.
4859 Sotter, J M, 47, Co C, died July 31.
3534 Southard, H, 5 cav, Co C, died July 18.
10526 Southard, N, 3, Co H, died Oct 6.
11846 Southard W A, 18, Co I, died Oct 23.
2877 Souther, Henry, 69, Co K, died July 4.
8124 Southworth, R, 39 cav, Co E, died Sept 9.
10468 Skall, S, 7 artll, Co L, died Oct 7.
13039 Steeley, T, 56, Co B, died Nov 15.
9954 Spark, G, 16 artll, Co C, died Sept 26.
6975 Sparks, E, 10, Co B, died Aug 27.
5431 Spaulding, H, 1 cav, Co F, died Aug 12.
5567 Spellman, John, 66, Co B, died Aug 13.
10712 Spencer, A, 93, Co D, died Feb 28.
10999 Sperry, A, 51, Co F, died Oct 16.
3583 Span, James, 147, Co H, died July 18.
5962 Spanbury, S, 14 artll, Co C, died Aug 17.
5521 Sprague, E H, 10 battery, died Aug 16.
3593 Sprague, J, 85, Co I, died July 19.
10730 Sprig, James A, 34 cav, Co E, died Oct 11.
4877 Sprink, A, 146, Co F, died Aug 6.
9035 Strata, John, 15, Co A, died Sept 17.
869 Stacey, John, 99, Co I, died May 4.
4574 Stadler, J, 39, Co A, died Aug 3.
10078 Stancliff, A B, 106, Co H, died Sept 30.
2370 Stanton, H H, 22, Co E, died June 27.
5187 Stark, J D, 100, Co A, died Aug 9.
11740 Starkweather, L, 146, Co E, died Nov 2.
13650 Star, C, 15, Co D, died Feb 13.
7881 Stanton, L H, 7 artll, Co K, died Aug 31.
3530 Stark, J H, 121, Co A, died June 26.
1696 Stanley, J C, 65, Co C, died June 7.
10290 St Dennis, L, 16, Co F, died Oct 4.
9903 Stewart, Peter, 5, Co B, died Sept 27.

31.
5076 Tanner, M, 1, Co E, died July 25.
4226 Tanschivit, Md, 15 artll, Co E, died July 30.
7019 Tell, Wm, 50, Co C, died Aug 27.
9143 Thompson, A, 9, Co D, died Sept 18.
133 Terry, Aaron, 12, Co K, died March 24.
9004 Tenevoh, M, 14 artll, Co E, died Sept 17.
4900 Tewey, J, 99, Co H, died Aug 6.
6445 Terwilliger, D R, 85, Co D, died Aug 23.
10459 Thomas, J, 2 cav, Co D, died Oct 5.
3508 Thomas, H, 89, Co D, died July 19.
3711 Thomas, W, 3, Co H, died July 21.
4619 Thomas, J, 85, Co G, died Aug 3.
10361 Thearer, J, 1 battery, died Oct 5.
8161 Thompson, C W, 85, Co K, died Sept 8.
4781 Thompson, J, 39, Co H, died Aug 5.
5510 Thompkins, Ira, 6 art, died Aug 13.
5524 Thompson, P, 10, Co E, died Aug 13.
6730 Thompson, N B, 146, Co A, died Aug 24.
5784 Thompson, J, 104, Co G, died Aug 15.
2613 Thompson, T, 12 cav, Co F, died June 23.
320 Thompson, Daniel, 142, Co E, died April 3.
3538 Thresh, G, 5 cav, Co K, died July 18.
5147 Thruston, N E, 85, Co C, died Aug 9.
11235 Thornton, J, 14 art, Co L, died Oct 21.
6509 Thorpe, W C, 83, Co I, died Aug 20.
4298 Thurston, G W, 85, Co E, died July 31.
12843 Thayer, G, 70, Co E, died April 22, '65.
679 Thierbach, P M, 39, Co D, died April 22.
11230 Tilton, H, 24 artll, died Oct 20.
3288 Tillitson, N P, 51, Co A, died Sept 9.
8849 Timerson, Wm, 7 artll, Co I, died Sept 15.
3680 Timmish, —, 85, Co C, died June 30.
659 Tiner, David, 79, Co E, died April 21.
10422 Townsend, W, 111, Co B, died Oct 6.
8063 Townsend, L, 23 cav, Co G, died Sept 7.
3683 Townsend, John, 52, Co A, died July 24.
525 Townsend, Geo M, 111, Co F, died April 14.
9080 Tobinson, E, 22, died Sept 17.
4774 Tobey, L, 100, Co D, died Aug 5.
10737 Tolal, Pat, 164, Co K, died Oct 11.
5833 Tonner, L, 5 cav, Co G, died Aug 16.
6047 Tobias, A, 120, Co G, died Aug 16.
2112 Toomey, J F, 85, Co I, died June 17.
13465 Tourney, P, 99, Co B, died Jan 16, '65.

List of New York Union Soldiers buried at Andersonville, contd.

76

Bibliography

Birth Records, Clay County, Illinois
(These revealed Louisa Andrews' maiden name,
birthplaces of both she and her husband.)

Boatner, Mark Mayo III. THE CIVIL WAR DICTIONARY.
New York: David McKay Company, Inc.

Cemetery Inscriptions, Clay County, Illinois.
Larkinburg Twp., Keen Chapel Cemetery, page
85.

Cromie, Alice Hamilton. A TOUR GUIDE TO THE CIVIL
WAR. 1964.

Hicken, Victor. ILLINOIS IN THE CIVIL WAR. Urbana:
University of Illinois Press, 1966.

ILLINOIS' ADJUTANT GENERAL'S REPORT, Volume II.
Springfield, IL. 1902.

Illinois Department of Public Health Death Index
1916 to 1942.

Illinois State Archives, Springfield, Illinois.
(Their records did not indicate that Samuel
Andrews was a prisoner of war.)

International Genealogical Index, the Church of
Jesus Christ of the Latter Day Saints, state
of Illinois microfiche, published 1994.

Randall, J.G. THE CIVIL WAR AND RECONSTRUCTION.
Boston: Little, Brown and Company, 1969.

United States Census, 1870 and 1880 Clay County,
Illinois, Larkinburg Twp.

Index

Note: This index includes the introduction and the privates that served in Company E 17th Illinois with Samuel Andrews.

Lavine, August
Levan, Charles
Miles, John A.
Moore, Rufus H.
Musser, Henry
Morton, Romain
Matheny, Reuben
Miles, John W.
Newton, Walter
Ostron, John H.
Olson, Charles
Perry, Reuben
Potter, Andrew J.
Price, Herschel C.
Rose, Albert
Samuels, John D.
Simcox, Robert
Stokes, Horace
Slawson, Rufus L.
Stotts, Harrison C.
Sallee, Benjamin F.
Saner, George W.
Slawson, Rufus L.
Stokes, Horace
Swanson, A. Swan
Spinney, Joseph F.
Thompson, Alexander
Tucker, John H.
Temple, John
Van Bremer, Benj.
Vertrees, Charles M.
Walker, Thomas R.
West, Julius B.
Wooten, Robert
Weamer, Frederick

Note: Freeman Parsons, recruit, only one in company E Illinois archives records as being prisoner of war.

7th Indiana infantry   43
7th Indiana calvary   51
4th Iowa reg.   39,55
9th Minnesota calvary   51
40th New Hampshire reg. 34

Newspaper article from

Chebanse, Illinois, October 16, 1908

Ex-Prisoners of War Reunion.

The 29th annual reunion of the Illinois Association of Union Ex-Prisoners of War will be held at White Hall, Green Co., Ill., Wednesday and Thursday Oct. 21st and 22nd. All Union ex-Prisoners of war who were taken prisoner in the Civil War from 1861 to 65 who were in prison sixty days or more and were open and honorably discharged from service are eligible to membership. There are no dues or fees for joining and all Union Ex-prisoners of war are invited to attend the meeting at White Hall and become members of this association. These meetings are held solely for purposes of keeping alive the social and fraternal spirit among the men who endured the privations of war and hardships and tortures of Hell in Andersonville, Libby, Florence, Cahawaba and other southern prisons that this country might remain united.

These meetings are attended by many who were not prisoners or even members of the Union Army during the War of the Rebellion as lessons in patriotism are taught by recital of experiences of those who endured the tyrannies of Wirz and Gen. Winder. The evening meeting is devoted to reminiscent talks by ex-prisoners.

The people of White Hall have made elaborate preparations for entertainment of visitors. All ex-prisoners are entertained by citizens free. All ex-prisoners are cordially invited to attend this meeting and they will be royally entertained.

Dr. and Mrs. W. H. Watson will attend this meeting.

Other Heritage Books by Helen Cox Tregillis:

Ancestors: A Teaching Story Using the Families of Cox, Hayes, Hulse, Range, Worley and Others with Suggested Lessons

Central Illinois Chronicles, Volumes 1-3

Illinois, the 14th Colony: French Period

Indians of Illinois

People and Rural Schools of Shelby County, Illinois

River Roads to Freedom: Fugitive Slave Notices and Sheriff Notices Found in Illinois Sources

The Native Tribes of Ohio